THE RULE AND EXERCISES OF HOLY LIVING

The Rule and Exercises of **Holy Living**

by Jeremy Taylor DD

abridged with a preface by Anne Lamb

foreword by Henry Chadwick
Dean of Christ Church
Oxford

HARPER & ROW, PUBLISHERS
NEW YORK AND EVANSTON
By arrangement with the Langford Press, England

Set in 11 pt Monotype Joanna 2 pt leaded
Designed by John Saville MSIA
Frontispiece by Peter Branfield MSIA

This abridged edition first published 1970 by the Langford Press, England.

THE RULES AND EXERCISES OF HOLY LIVING. *Copyright © 1970 by Kenneth Langford and Ronald Goff. All rights reserved. Printed in the United States of America. No part of this book may be used or reproduced in any manner whatsoever without written permission except in the case of brief quotations embodied in critical articles and reviews. For information address Harper & Row, Publishers, Inc., 49 East 33rd Street, New York, N.Y. 10016.*

FIRST UNITED STATES EDITION

LIBRARY OF CONGRESS CATALOG CARD NUMBER: 76-141658

Contents

Foreword

A great classic of the spiritual life needs no impertinent commendation or appearance of patronage. Jeremy Taylor's book remains a living masterpiece by its shrewd insight, sense of proportion, wide sympathy, and serene freedom from disputatious controversy. Writing at the time of the English civil war, Taylor sensed both the alienation of his seventeenth century contemporaries from a religion that was becoming associated with conspiracy and strife, and also the isolation of individuals deprived of spiritual help. He wrote for an Anglicanism not only disestablished but actively persecuted, for a church in the wilderness, despised and rejected, lacking all the signs of social success and acceptance. Yet throughout his book there is no breath of resentment or sad and wistful conservatism.

Some part of the book's living power derives from the open and liberal spirit of its author. Characteristically, Jeremy Taylor's Christian humanism never found deeper expression than here. He drew not only on the Bible and the tradition of catholic spirituality, but also on the great moralists of the ancient world, especially Plutarch and Seneca. He and his intended readers shared a common education in the literature of Greece and Rome, so that he was free to illustrate his points with instances and anecdotes taken from a vast library of literature stretching from Homer to his own day. Yet this frequent reference to the classical world, which helped him to gain an audience in the seventeenth century, may lose him one in the twentieth.

Anne Lamb's abridgement has been done with the greatest possible tact and sensitivity. She has kept some of the more telling classical aphorisms and anecdotes. But necessarily and rightly she has sacrificed many of the more erudite allusions which are today a barrier to the general reader. Even in this shortened form, *Holy Living* remains a substantial treatise. Nothing essential to the whole has been lost, and in this form one of the most remarkable books of the Christian tradition may find many new readers.

HENRY CHADWICK
Oxford, July 1970

Preface

Holiness is not a conscious preoccupation commonly spoken of today. What then of a new edition of *The Rule and Exercises of Holy Living*, such a comprehensive and uncompromising title? Is it not irrelevant as an outdated concept, frighteningly totalitarian in its approach to morals, or is it just impractical idealism? Yet we find ourselves longing for a quality of life which is the finest and best of which we are capable, both for the sake of those we love and care for, and for our actions to display faithfulness to our best aspirations and values. Wholeness, making the most of life, success in our projects, fulfilment of our hopes, joy and delight in our relationships and experience, and the discovery of some basis for recognising and affirming that there is both sense and purpose in it, despite all that seems to conspire against such belief or to destroy such hope. Individuals still face life with bewildered agony, vulnerable to its tragedy, searching for a sense of identity, value and relevance, and for some vision which will give meaning to existence.

In our own times, the search expresses itself more often in the language of psychology, economics and political ideology than in that of theology and philosophy, but the searcher is just as much left with the responsibility of accepting, rejecting or of simply sitting on the fence: (becoming involved, opting out or remaining disengaged). The extension of knowledge and of human consciousness does not alter this predicament. It intensifies the potentialities of life in what would have seemed unrealisable dreams to previous generations, and somehow this adds to the burden of responsibility and the fear of failure as we confront the perennial issues. If holiness is really about the concern and need of people to find wholeness, to realise themselves, be healed of inadequacies and infirmities, and to enable us to cope with the possibilities and responsibilities of life more fully, then it is neither outdated nor irrelevant. It is concerned with the longing to find out what life is for, and the mind and will of that for which we are created (for the believer, that of the Creator) and to know and follow it. 'Thy kingdom come, thy will be done.' It affirms a way of life which aspires to the best.

Jeremy Taylor tasted the extremities of human experience in his short but eventful life (1613–67). A brilliantly gifted and handsome youth, with the diligence to do justice to the splendid opportunities of his Cambridge boyhood and education, his success seemed assured. B.A. in 1631, ordained and M.A. by 1633 when he found himself in the pulpit of St. Paul's Cathedral, deputising for a friend too ill to keep the appointment; 'His graceful person and elocution, together with the varied richness of his style and argument and, perhaps, the singularity of a theological lecturer of twenty years of age, very soon obtained him friends and admirers.' (Heber). He was summoned by Archbishop Laud to preach at Lambeth and nominated to a fellowship at All Souls, became Rector of Uppingham and Chaplain to King Charles I, and a husband and father. But, by the age of thirty, he was deprived of his living, and subsequently faced with poverty, imprisonment and repeated personal bereavement, including the loss of four of his sons in infancy or childhood.

The faith upon which his life was built and which he so effectively proclaimed in prosperity, sustained him in his sorrows and reverses of fortune, and wrought in him the conviction that the religion of Christ is pre-eminently concerned with individual goodness, that is to say, personal holiness. Not that this implied neglect of the need for established order. His first published work, *Episcopacy Asserted*, was rewarded with the degree of Doctor of Divinity conferred by King Charles himself, probably at Oxford in 1642, and clearly identified

him as unsympathetic to the Parliamentary Party. He was in prison
at Cardigan in 1644 and then followed the years of exile, poverty and
obscurity in Wales. He existed by keeping a school with two friends at
Llanfihangel, near the estate of Lord Carbery at Golden Grove where
he was befriended and welcomed and invited to minister as domestic
chaplain. That his interest should fasten on the question of freedom of
conscience and religious toleration is not surprising. The resulting
book, *The Liberty of Prophesying*, must have cleared his mind on this
fundamental matter, and been of great value to him when, after the
Restoration, he became Bishop of Down, Connor and Dromore, and
was confronted with a situation fraught with bigotry and extremism.
It has been described as a very Anglican book. He insists that toleration is not indifference, and that its object is, in the first instance, not
truth but peace. He had learned that 'If you, for conscience sake, do
them wrong, they will hate both you and your religion' and that
'The way to cure the inconvenience is to alter the man, not change the
institution'.

The patronage of Lord Carbery, the friendship of Frances, Lady
Carbery, his responsibilities as chaplain to their household and the
task of teaching, enabled Taylor to transform the years of exile into a
most creative period. After *The Liberty of Prophesying* he wrote some
studies in the life of Christ entitled *The Great Exemplar* and its popularity
encouraged him to follow it with a Short Catechism for Children
which he later revised and published as *The Golden Grove*. Then came
Holy Living, 1650–51, probably the best known of all his works, which
was written at the desire and for the use of Lady Carbery. In the dedi-
cation, Taylor describes his hopes for the usefulness of his book, in
the context of these troubled times. The sustenance and encouragement of someone who so valued his teaching and ministry and shared
with him the same wholehearted seriousness and devotion in the
pursuit of holiness must have been very great. Having borne ten
children in thirteen years of marriage, maintained a great household
in times of revolution and civil war and lived in a way which offered
inspiration for what became a devotional classic of the English language and Church, Lady Carbery died. *Holy Dying*, often in the past
published in one volume with Holy Living, was finished shortly

afterwards and had been intended 'to minister to her piety'.

To abridge is to interfere with the author's original work and requires justification. This edition is less than half the length of the text of Heber and Edens' (Longmans, 1856) and is not for the scholar. It would be an exaggeration to compare a study of the original to an archaeological dig, unless the site was quite exceptionally rich, for the treasures of piety and the glorious language in which they are often expressed are not few or far between. But Taylor did believe in driving his points home by repetition, and in any case, brevity was not then held to be the virtue in religious discourse as in our own concentrated and impatient days. Every word is his (though many are left out), and the utmost care has been taken to retain his balance of emphasis as well as the form and rhythm of his phrasing. Occasionally the cuts have required an adjustment of punctuation, a comma becomes a full stop and a sentence must commence with a capital letter. His addiction to colon and semi-colon is apparent. Coleridge described the style of Taylor's sentences as 'thought agglomerating flood' and C. J. Stranks in *The Life and Writings of Jeremy Taylor* (S.P.C.K., 1952) says : 'Long as are the sentences . . . their length in no way obscures their meaning . . . It would be quite possible to repunctuate Taylor's works, and, without altering a single word, reduce his sentences to a modern brevity'. The table of contents, chapter headings and sub-headings are all there but are sometimes also abridged. A few of the original prayers and exercises have been left out, and those included more drastically reduced than the rest of the text. Taylor's devotions overflowed into an effusion and length, yet contain a fundamental form and feeling which could as well be used to refresh public worship as they may inspire and enrich private prayer, according to his intention. Scriptural references are given in endnotes as and when they appear, but the many classical references, obscure today except to the specialist, have been left out.

Jeremy Taylor believed of the Christian religion that it is 'As eternal as the soul of man, and can no more cease than our spirits can die . . . and is the perfection of the soul, the highest reason of man, and the glorification of God'. Heber, after exhaustive study of his life and works, says, of his humanity : 'No writer, with whose works I am acquainted, has spoken more wisely or with greater knowledge of the human heart'.

The findings of this literary and devotional dig are not, therefore, relics and remains, interesting and consequential only as a key to understanding an extinct way of life. They state the Christian vision of how to live with a vigorously individual and practical ring which suits the mood of our realistic times, as impatient with optimistic illusion as with rigid moral formulae. His reflections are so full of common sense, sympathetic insight and sound judgement, deeply conscious of the gap between discerning and knowing what we ought to do and finding the will and strength to do it, and sure that this is available in the transforming power of love. He summed it up in the course of a sermon preached, late in his life, to the University of Dublin:

'The way to judge of religion, is by doing of our duty; and theology is rather a divine life than a divine knowledge. In heaven, indeed, we must first see and then love; but here, on earth, we must first love, and love will open our eyes as well as our hearts; and we shall then see, and perceive and understand'.

ANNE LAMB

The Rule and Exercises of Holy Living

in which are described the means and instruments of
obtaining every virtue,

and the remedies against
every vice,

and considerations serving to the
resisting of all temptations.

Together with Prayers containing the whole
duty of a Christian

and the parts of devotion fitted to
all occasions, and furnished for
all necessities.

To The Right Honourable Richard Lord Vaughan

Earl of Carbery, Knight of the Honourable Order of the Bath.

My Lord
I have lived to see religion painted upon banners, and thrust out of churches, and the temple turned into a tabernacle, and God to be worshipped, not as He is, the Father of our Lord Jesus, the King of sufferings; nor as the God of peace; but rather as the Lord of hosts, which title He was pleased to lay aside when the kingdom of the gospel was preached by the Prince of peace. But when religion puts on armour, it may have the power of the sword, but not the power of godliness, and we have no remedy but the fellowship of Christ's sufferings, and the returns of the God of peace. Men are apt to prefer a prosperous error before an afflicted truth; and that those few who have no other plot in their religion but to serve God and save their souls, do want such assistance of ghostly counsel as may assist their endeavours in the acquist of virtues, and relieve their dangers when they are tempted to sin and death; I thought I had reasons enough inviting me to draw into one body those advices: that a collection of holy precepts and the rules for conduct might be committed to a book, which they might always have; since they could not always

have a prophet at their needs, nor be suffered to go up to the house of the Lord.

I know, my lord, that there are some who add scorn to the afflictions of the Church of England, and because her solemn assemblies are scattered, think that the religion is lost, and the church divorced from God. Because we now want the blessings of external communion, and of a prosperous and unafflicted people, we are to take estimate of ourselves, and every man is to give sentence concerning the state of his own soul, by the essential parts of religion rather than by the uncertain significations of any exterior adherencies; for though it be uncertain, when a man is the member of a church, whether he be a member of Christ or no, because in the church's net there are fishes good and bad; yet we may be sure that if we be members of Christ, we are of a church to all purposes of spiritual religion and salvation.

A man does certainly belong to God who believes and is baptized into all the articles of the Christian faith, and studies to improve his knowledge in the matters of God, so as may best make him to live a holy life; he that, in obedience to Christ, worships God diligently, frequently, and constantly, with natural religion, that is of prayer, praises, and thanksgiving; he that takes all opportunities to remember Christ's death by a frequent sacrament, as it can be had, or else by inward acts of understanding, will and memory (which is spiritual communion) supplies the want of the external rite; he that lives chastely; and is merciful; and despises the world, using it as a man, but never suffering it to rifle a duty; and is just in his dealing, and diligent in his calling; he that is humble in spirit; and obedient to government; and is content in his fortune and employment; he that does his duty because he loves God; and especially if after all this he be afflicted, and patient, or prepared to suffer affliction for the cause of God: the man that has these twelve signs of grace does as certainly belong to God, and is His son as surely, as he is His creature.

These are the marks of the Lord Jesus, and the characters of a Christian: this is a good religion; and these things God's grace hath put into our powers, and God's laws have made to be our duty, and the nature of man, and the needs of commonwealths, have made to be necessary. The other accidents and pomps of a church are things without our power, and are not in our choice; they are good to be used when they may be had, and they help to illustrate or advantage it: yet they are not of its constitution as it is Christian, and hopes to be saved.

And now the case is so with us that we are reduced to that religion which no man can forbid; which we can keep in the midst of a persecution; that by which we can be servants of God, and receive the spirit of Christ, and make use of His comforts, and live in His love and in charity with all men. I have told what men ought to do, and by what means they may be assisted, with as much quickness as I could think necessary to establish a rule. In the use of which rules, although they are plain, useful, and fitted for the best and worst understandings, and for the need of all men, yet I shall desire the reader to proceed with the following advices.

First, they that will with profit make use of the proper instruments of virtue, must so live as if they were always under the physician's hand. For the counsels of religion are not to be applied to the distempers of the soul as men used to take hellebore; but they must dwell together with the spirit of a man, and be twisted about his understanding forever: they must be used like nourishment, that is by a daily care and meditation; not like a single medicine, and upon the actual pressure of a present necessity. For counsels and wise discourses applied to an actual distemper, at the best are but like strong smells to an epileptic person; sometimes they may raise him, but they never cure him. The following rules, if they be made familiar to our natures and the thoughts of every day, may make virtue and religion become easy and habitual; but when the temptation is present, and hath already seized upon some portions of our consent, we are not so apt to be counselled, and we find no gust or relish in the precept; the lessons are the same but the instrument is unstrung or out of tune.

Secondly, in using the instruments of virtue, we must distinguish instruments from duties, and prudent advices from necessary injunctions; and if by any other means the duty can be secured, let there be no scruples stirred. For there are some persons in whom the Spirit of God hath breathed so bright a flame of love, that they do all

their acts of virtue by perfect choice and without objection, and their
zeal is warmer than that it will be allayed by temptation: and to such
persons mortification by philosophical instruments, as fasting, sackcloth, and other rudenesses to the body is wholly useless; it is always
a more uncertain means to acquire any virtue, or secure any duty; and
if love hath filled all the corners of our soul, it alone is able to do all
the work of God.

Thirdly, where the duty is necessary, and means reasonable, dispute
not too busily whether in all circumstances it can fit thy particular;
but make use of it. For it is a good sign of a great religion, and no
imprudence, when we have sufficiently considered the substance of
affairs, then to be easy, humble, obedient, apt, and credulous. He that
gives alms, does best to give freely, incuriously and abundantly. A
man must not weigh grains in the accounts of his repentance; but for
a great sin have a great sorrow, and a great severity; arithmetical
measures, especially of our own proportioning, are but arguments of
want of love or else are instruments of scruple, and then become
dangerous. Use the rule heartily and enough, and there will be no
harm in thy error, if any should happen.

Fourthly, if thou intendest heartily to serve God and avoid sin,
refuse not the hardest and most severe advice in order to it; for whatsoever it is, custom will make it easy.

Fifthly, when many instruments for obtaining any virtue, or restraining any vice are propounded, observe which of them fits thy
person or thy need, and use it; that thou mayest be engaged to watch,
and use spiritual arts and observation about thy soul. As the interest
is greater, so the necessities are more, and the cases more intricate,
and the accidents and dangers greater and more importunate; and
there is greater skill required than in the securing an estate, or restor-
ing health to an infirm body. I wish all men in the world did heartily
believe so much of this as is true; it would very much help to do the
work of God.

I am,

In the deepest sense of duty and affection,

Your honour's most obliged and most humble servant:

JER. TAYLOR

1 · Introduction on the general means serving to a holy life

It is necessary that every man should consider, that since God hath given him an excellent nature, wisdom and choice, an understanding soul and an immortal spirit, having made him lord over the beasts and but a little lower than the angels; He hath also appointed for him a work and a service great enough to employ those abilities, and hath also designed him to a state of life after this, to which he can only arrive by that service and obedience. And therefore as every man is wholly God's own portion by the title of creation, so all our labours and care, all our powers and faculties, must be wholly employed in the service of God, and even all the days of our life.

Neither is it sufficient that we think of the service of God as a work of the least necessity, or of small employment, but that it be done by us as God intended it; and with great earnestness and passion, with much zeal and desire; that we refuse no labour; that we bestow upon it much time; that we use the best guides, and arrive at the end of glory by all the ways of grace, of prudence and religion.

And, indeed, if we consider how much of our lives is taken up by the needs of nature; how many years are wholly spent, before we come to any use of reason; how many years more, before that reason is useful to us to any great purposes; how imperfect our discourse is made by our evil education, false principles, ill company, bad examples, and want of experience; how many parts of our wisest and best years are spent in eating and sleeping, in necessary businesses and unnecessary vanities, in worldly civilities and less useful circumstances, that little portion of hours that is left for the practices of piety and religious walking with God, is so short and trifling, that, were not the goodness of God infinitely great, it might seem unreasonable or impossible for us to expect of Him eternal joys in heaven.

And although we scatter much, yet we gather but little profit: but from prayer and the exercises of a pious life the return is great and profitable; and what we sow in the minutes and spare portions of a few years, grows up to crowns and sceptres in a happy and a glorious eternity.

1. Therefore, although the greatest part of our time cannot be spent in the direct actions of devotion and religion, yet it will become not only a duty, but also a great providence, to lay aside for the services of God as much as we can; because God rewards our minutes with long and eternal happiness; and 'no man is a better merchant than he that lays out his time upon God, and his money upon the poor'.

2. God hath not only permitted us to serve the necessities of our nature, but hath made them to become parts of our duty; that if we, by directing these actions to the glory of God, intend them as instruments to continue our persons in His service, He may turn our nature into grace, and accept our natural actions as actions of religion. God is pleased if we eat or drink temperately, and as best may preserve our health, that our health may enable our services towards Him. And there is no one minute of our lives (after we are come to the use of reason), but we are or may be doing the work of God, even then when we most of all serve ourselves.

3. In these and all other actions of our lives we always stand before God, acting and speaking, and thinking in His presence, that it matters not that our conscience is sealed with secrecy, since it lies open to God.

These three considerations rightly managed will be like Elisha stretched upon the child, apt to put life and quickness into every part of it, and to make us live the life of grace, and do the work of God.

I shall reduce these three to practice, and shew how every Christian may improve all and each of these to the advantage of piety in the whole course of his life; that if he please to bear but one of them upon his spirit, he may feel the benefit, like an universal instrument, helpful in all spiritual and temporal actions.

I CARE OF OUR TIME

He that is choice of his time will also be choice of his company, and choice of his actions: lest he be throwing his time and himself away.

God hath given to man a short time here upon earth, and yet upon this eternity depends: so that, for every hour of our life (after we are persons capable of laws, and know good from evil) we must give account to the great Judge of men and angels. And this is it which our blessed Saviour told us, that we must account for every idle word; not meaning that every word which is not designed to edification, or is less prudent, shall be reckoned for a sin; but that the time which we spend in our idle talking and unprofitable discoursings, might and ought to have been employed to spiritual and useful purposes.

For we must remember that we have a great work to do, many enemies to conquer, many evils to prevent, much danger to run through, many difficulties to be mastered, many necessities to serve and much good to do, many children to provide for, or many friends to support, or many poor to relieve, or many diseases to cure, besides the needs of nature and of relation, our private and our public cares, and duties of the world which necessity and the providence of God hath adopted into the family of religion.

We must remember that the life of every man may be so ordered, and indeed must, that it may be a perpetual serving of God. For God provides the good things of the world to serve the needs of nature by the labours of the ploughman, the skill and pains of the artisan, and the dangers and traffic of the merchant: these men are, in their calling, the ministers of the Divine Providence, and the stewards of the creation, and servants of a great family of God, the world, in the employment of procuring necessaries for food and clothing, ornament and physic. In their proportions also a king and a priest and a prophet, a judge and an advocate, doing the works of their employment according to their proper rules, are doing the work of God. So that no man can complain that his calling takes him off from religion; his calling itself, and his employment in honest trades and offices is a serving of God; and if it be moderately pursued, and according to the rules of Christian prudence, will leave void spaces enough for prayers and retirements of a more spiritual religion.

God hath given every man work enough to do, that there shall be no room for idleness; and yet that there shall be space for devotion. He that hath the fewest businesses of the world, is called upon to spend more time in the dressing of his soul; and he that hath the most affairs, may so order them that they shall be a service of God; blessed with prayers and actions of religion, and all day long hallowed by a holy intention.

However, so long as idleness is quite shut out from our lives, all the sins of wantonness are prevented, and there is but little room left for temptation; to a busy man temptation is fain to climb up together with his businesses, and sins creep upon him only by accidents and occasions: whereas to an idle person they come in a full body, and with open violence, and the impudence of a restless importunity.

Idleness is called 'the sin of Sodom and her daughters'[1] and indeed is 'the burial of a living man'; an idle person being so useless to any purposes of God and man, that he is like one that is dead, unconcerned in the changes and necessities of the world; and he only lives to spend his time, and eat the fruits of the earth: like a vermin or a wolf; when their time comes they die and perish, and in the meantime do no good; they neither plough nor carry burdens; all that they do either is unprofitable or mischievous.

Idleness is the greatest prodigality in the world: it throws away that which is invaluable in respect of its present use, and irreparable, when it is past, being to be recovered by no power of art or nature.

To secure and improve our time, we may practice in the following rules:

Rules for employing our time

1. In the morning when you awake, accustom yourself to think first upon God, or something in order to His service; and at night also, let Him close thine eyes: and let your sleep be necessary and healthful, not idle beyond the needs and conveniences of nature; and sometimes be curious to see the preparation which the sun makes when he is coming forth from his chambers of the east.

2. Let every man that hath a calling be diligent in pursuance of its employment.

3. Let all the intervals or void spaces of time be employed in prayers, reading, meditating, works of nature, recreation, charity, friendliness and neighbourhood, and means of spiritual and corporal health. But begin and end the day with God, with such forms of devotion as shall be proper to our necessities.

4. The resting days of Christians, and festivals of the Church, must in no sense be days of idleness; for it is better to plough upon holy days, than to do nothing, or to do viciously: but let them be spent in the works of the day, that is, of religion and charity.

5. Avoid the company of drunkards and busy-bodies, and all such as are apt to talk much to little purpose: for no man can be provident of his time, that is not prudent in the choice of his company; and if one of the speakers be vain, tedious, and trifling, he that hears, and he that answers, in the discourse, are equal losers of their time.

6. Never walk with any man, or undertake any trifling employment, merely to pass the time away: for every day well spent may become a 'day of salvation', and time rightly employed is an 'acceptable time'.

7. In the midst of the works of thy calling, often retire to God in short prayers; for so thou reconcilest the outward work and thy inward calling, the Church and the Commonwealth, the employment of the body and the interest of thy soul; for be sure that God is present at thy breathings and hearty sighings of prayer, as soon as at the longer offices of less busied persons.

8. Let your employment be such as may become a reasonable person; and not be a business fit for children or distracted people, but fit for your age and understanding. For a man may be very idly busy, and take great pains to so little purpose, that in his labours and expense of time, he shall serve no end but of folly and vanity. There are some trades that wholly serve the ends of idle persons and fools, and such as are fit to be seized upon by the severity of laws, and banished from under the sun; and there are some people who are busy, but it is as Domitian was, in catching flies.

9. Let your employment be fitted to your person and calling. Some there are that employ their time in affairs infinitely below the dignity of their person; and being called by God, or by the republic, to help to bear great burdens, and to judge a people, do enfeeble their understandings and disable their persons by sordid and brutish business. Thus Nero went up and down Greece, and challenged the fiddlers at their trade. Aeropus, a Macedonian king, made lanterns; Harcatius, the king of Parthia, was a mole-catcher; and Biantes, the Lydian, filed needles. He that is appointed to minister in holy things must not suffer secular affairs and sordid arts to eat up great portions of his employment; a clergyman must not keep a tavern, nor a judge be an innkeeper.

10. Let our employment be such as becomes a Christian; that is, in no sense, mingled with sin: for he that takes pains to serve the ends of covetousness, or ministers to another's lust, or keeps a shop of impurities or intemperance, is idle in the worst sense.

11. Persons of great quality, and of no trade, are to be most prudent and careful in their employment and traffic of time. They are miserable if their education hath been so loose and undisciplined as to leave them unfurnished of skill to spend their time; but most miserable are they, if such misgovernment and unskilfulness make them fall into vicous and baser company. They that are learned know the worth of time, and the manner how well to improve a day; for such purposes in which they may be most useful in order to arts or arms, to counsel in public, or government in their country. But for others of them that are unlearned, let them choose good company, such as may not tempt them to a vice, but that may supply their defects

by way of conduct or conversation. Let them learn easy and useful things, read history and the laws of the land, learn the customs of their country, the condition of their own estate, profitable and charitable contrivances of it: let them study prudently to govern their families, learn the burdens of their tenants, the necessities of their neighbours, and in their proportion supply them, and reconcile their enmities, and prevent their lawsuits or quickly end them; and in this glut of leisure and disemployment, let them set apart greater portions of their time for religion and the necessities of their souls.

1 2. Let women of noble birth and great fortunes do the same things in their proportions and capacities, nurse their children, look to the affairs of the house, visit poor cottages, and relieve their necessities; be courteous to the neighbourhood, learn of their husbands or their spiritual guides, read good books, pray often and 'learn to do good works for necessary uses'.

1 3. Let all persons of all conditions avoid misspendings of their time, while they dress and comb out all their opportunities of their morning devotion, and half the day's severity, and sleep out the care and provision for their souls.

1 4. Let every one of every condition avoid curiosity, and all inquiry into things that concern them not. For they concern us, as one member is concerned in the grief of another; but going from house to house, tattlers and busybodies, which are the canker and rust of idleness, as idleness is the rust of time, are reproved by the apostle in severe language, and forbidden in order to this exercise.

1 5. As much as may be, cut off all impertinent and useless employments of your life, unnecessary and fantastic visits, long waitings upon great personages, where neither duty, nor necessity, nor charity oblige us; all vain meetings, all laborious trifles, and whatsoever spends much time to no real, civil, religious, or charitable purpose.

1 6. Let not your recreations be lavish spenders of your time; but choose such as are healthful, short, transient, recreative, and apt to refresh you; but at no hand dwell upon them, or make them your great employment: for he that spends his time in sports, and calls it recreation, is like him whose garment is all made of fringes, and his meat nothing but sauces. And therefore avoid such games as require

much time or which are apt to steal thy affections from more severe employments. For to whatsoever thou hast given thy affection, thou wilt not grudge to give thy time. Natural necessity and the example of St. John who recreated himself by sporting with a tame partridge, teach us, that it is lawful to relax and unbend our bow, but not to suffer it to be unready or unstrung.

17. Set apart some portions of every day for more solemn devotion which be severe in observing : and if variety of employment, or prudent affairs, or civil society, press upon you, and may make prayers shorter, yet let nothing but a violent, sudden, and impatient necessity make thee wholly to omit thy morning and evening devotions.

18. Do not the 'work of God negligently'[2] and idly : let not thy heart be upon the world when thy hand is lifted up in prayer. Sir Thomas More, being sent for by the king when he was at his prayers in public, returned answer, he would attend him when he had first performed his service to the King of kings. In honouring God and doing His work, put forth all thy strength.

19. It is good that devotion be the measure of your time : that those spaces, which have in them no direct business of the world, may be filled with religion.

20. Be sure by a timely diligence 'to redeem the time'; that is, to be pious and religious in those cases in which formerly you have sinned.

21. Let him that is most busied set apart some solemn time every year,[3] in which, quitting all worldly business, he may attend wholly to fasting and prayer, and the dressing of his soul by confessions, meditations, and attendances upon God; that he may make up his accounts, renew his vows, make amends for his carelessness, from whence levity and the vanities of the world, or the opportunity of temptations, or the distraction of secular affairs, have carried him.

22. In this we shall be much assisted if, before we sleep every night we examine the actions of the past day with a particular scrutiny, if there have been any accident extraordinary, as long discourse, a feast, much business, variety of company. If nothing but common hath happened, the less examination will suffice ; only let us take care

that we sleep not without such a recollection of the actions of the day, either to be the matter of sorrow or thanksgiving.

23. Let all these things be done prudently and moderately, not with scruple and vexation. These are good advantages, but not divine commandments, to be used as shall be found expedient to every one's condition. The duty consists not scrupulously in minutes and half-hours, but in greater portions of time; provided that no minute be employed in sin; and some portion of every day, be allowed for religion.

The benefits of this care of our time

This exercise, besides that it hath influence upon our whole lives, hath a special efficacy for the preventing of those sins which idleness and beggary usually betray men to; such as are lying, flattery, stealing, and dissimulation. Secondly, it is a proper antidote against carnal sins, and such as proceed from fulness of bread and emptiness of employment. Thirdly, it is a great instrument of preventing the smallest sins and irregularities of our life, which usually creep upon idle, disemployed, and curious persons. Fourthly, it not only teaches us to avoid evil, but engages us upon doing good, as the proper business of all our days. Fifthly, it prepares us against sudden changes, for he that is curious of his time will not easily be unready and unfurnished.

II PURITY OF INTENTION

That we should intend and design God's glory in every action we do, whether it be natural or chosen, is expressed by St. Paul, 'Whether ye eat or drink, do all to the glory of God'.[4] Which rule when we observe, every action of nature becomes religious, and every meal is an act of worship as well as an act of prayer. Blessed be that goodness and grace of God which, out of infinite desire to glorify and save mankind, would make the very works of nature capable of becoming acts of virtue, that all our lifetime we may do Him service.

This grace is so excellent, that it sanctifies the most common action of our life; and yet so necessary, that without it the very best actions of our devotions are imperfect. For he that prays out of custom, or gives alms for praise, or fasts to be accounted religious, is but a pharisee in his devotion, and a beggar in his alms, and a hypocrite in his fast. But a holy end sanctifies all these and all other actions which can be made holy, and gives distinction to them, and procures acceptance.

For, as to know the end distinguishes a man from a beast, so to choose a good end distinguishes him from an evil man. Hezekiah repeated his good deeds upon his sick-bed, and obtained favour of God, but the pharisee was accounted insolent for doing the same thing; because this man did it to upbraid his brother, the other to obtain a mercy of God. Zacharias questioned with the angel about his message, and was made speechless for his incredulity; but the blessed Virgin Mary questioned too, and was blameless; for she did it to inquire after the manner of the thing, but he did not believe the thing itself: he doubted of God's power, or the truth of the messenger; but she, only of her own incapacity. This was it which distinguished the mourning of David from the exclamation of Saul; the tears of Peter from the repentance of Judas: for the praise is not in the deed done, but in the manner of its doing. If a man visits his sick friend, and watches at his pillow for charity's sake, and because of his old affection, we approve it; but if he does it in hope of legacy, he is a vulture, and only watches for the carcase. The same things are honest and dishonest: the manner of doing them, and the end of the design, makes the separation.

Holy intention is to the actions of a man that which the soul is to the body, or form to its matter, or the root to the tree, or the sun to the world, or the fountain to a river, or the base to a pillar: for without these the body is a dead trunk, the matter is sluggish, the tree is a block, the world is darkness, the river is quickly dry, the pillar rushes into flatness and a ruin; and the action is sinful, or unprofitable and vain. The poor farmer that gave a dish of cold water to Artaxerxes was rewarded with a golden goblet; and he that gives the same present to a disciple in the name of a disciple, shall have a crown; but if he gives water in despite, when the disciple needs wine or a cordial, his reward shall be to want that water to cool his tongue.

But this duty must be reduced to rules.

Rules for our intentions

1. In every action reflect upon the end; and in your undertaking it, consider why you do it, and what you propound to yourself for a reward, and to your action as its end.

2. Begin every action in the name of the Father, of the Son, and of the Holy Ghost; the meaning of which is: that we design it to the glory of God: and that it may be so blessed that what you intend for innocent and holy purposes, may not, by any chance, or abuse, or misunderstanding of men, be turned into evil, or made the occasion of sin.

3. Let every action be begun with prayer, that God would not only bless the action but sanctify your purpose.

4. In the prosecution of the action, renew and re-enkindle your purpose.

'Not unto us, O Lord, not unto us, but unto Thy Name let all praise be given': and consider,

'Now I am working the work of God: I am His servant, I am in a happy employment, I am doing my Master's business, I am not at my own dispose, I am using His talents, and all the gain must be His'.

5. Have a care, that, while the altar thus sends up a holy fume, thou dost not suffer the birds to come and carry away the sacrifice: that is, let not that which began well, and was intended for God's glory, decline and end in thy own praise, or temporal satisfaction, or a sin. A story, told to represent the vileness of unchastity, is well begun; but if thy female auditor be pleased with thy language, and begins rather to like thy person for thy story than to dislike the crime, be watchful, lest this goodly head of gold descend in silver and brass, and end in iron and clay, like Nebuchadnezzar's image; for from the end it shall have its name and reward.

6. If any accidental event, which was not first intended by thee, can come to pass, let it not be taken into thy purposes; but when the temptation is found out, turn all thy enmity upon that.

7. In every more solemn action of religion join together many good ends, that the consideration of them, may entertain all your affections; and that, when any one ceases, the purity of your intention may be supported by another supply. He that fasts only to tame

a rebellious body, when he is provided of a remedy either in grace or nature, may be tempted to leave off his fasting. But he that in his fast intends the mortification of every unruly appetite, and accustoming himself to bear the yoke of the Lord, will have reason enough to continue his purpose, and to sanctify it. And certain it is, the more good ends are designed in an action, the more degrees of excellency the man obtains.

8. If any temptation to spoil your purpose happens in a religious duty, do not presently omit the action, but rather strive to rectify your intention, and to mortify the temptation. St. Bernard taught us this rule: for when the Devil, observing him to preach excellently and to do much benefit to his hearers, tempted him to vain-glory, hoping that the good man, to avoid that, would cease preaching, he gave this answer only, 'I neither began for thee, neither for thee will I make an end'.

9. In all actions, offer yourself and all you do to God's glory.

10. Call not every temporal end a defiling of thy intention, but only when it contradicts any of the ends of God; or when it is principally intended in an action of religion. For sometimes a temporal end is part of our duty and calling, whether our employment be religious or civil. We are commanded to provide for our family: but if the minister of divine offices shall take upon him that holy calling for covetous or ambitious ends, he hath polluted his hands and his heart.

But because a man's heart may deceive him, and he may not well know what is in his own spirit; by these following signs we shall best make a judgment whether our intentions be pure and our purposes holy.

Signs of purity of intention

1. It is probable our hearts[5] are right with God, and our intentions innocent and pious, if we set upon actions of religion or civil life with an affection proportionate to the quality of the work. That we value a religious design before a temporal, when otherwise they are in equal order to their several ends: that is, that whatsoever is necessary in order to our soul's health be higher esteemed than what is for bodily; when we choose any temporal inconvenience, rather than

commit a sin, and when we choose to do a duty, rather than to get gain. But he that does his recreation or his merchandise cheerfully, promptly, readily, and busily, and the works of religion slowly, flatly, and without appetite, and the spirit moves like Pharaoh's chariots when the wheels were off; it is a sign that his heart is not right with God, but it cleaves too much to the world.

2. It is likely our hearts are pure, and our intentions spotless, when we are not solicitous of the opinion and censures of men; but only that we do our duty, and be accepted of God.

3. He that does as well in private, between God and his own soul, as in public, in pulpits, in theatres, and market-places, hath given himself a good testimony that his purposes are full of honesty, nobleness, and integrity. He, who is to be our judge, is better than ten thousand witnesses. But he that would have his virtue published, studies not virtue, but glory.

4. It is well also when we are not solicitous or troubled concerning the effect and event of all our actions; but that being first by prayer recommended to Him, is left at His disposal, we have nothing left to rest in but the honesty of our purposes.

5. He loves virtue for God's sake and its own that loves and honours it wherever it is to be seen; but he that is envious or angry at a virtue that is not his own, at the perfection or excellency of his neighbour, is not covetous of the virtue, but of its reward and reputation; and then his intentions are polluted. But he that desires only that the work of God and religion shall go on, is pleased with it, whosoever is the instrument.

6. He that despises the world is the most secured of his intentions, because he is the farthest removed from a temptation. In what degree we despise sensual pleasure, or secular honours, or worldly reputation, in the same degree we shall conclude our heart right to religion and spiritual designs.

7. He that is indifferent whether he serve God in riches or in poverty, is rather a seeker of God than of himself; and he that will throw away a good book because it is not curiously gilded, is more curious to please his eye that to inform his understanding.

8. When a temporal end consisting with a spiritual, and pretended

to be subordinate to it, happens to fail and be defeated, if we can rejoice in that, so God's glory may be secured; it is a great sign our hearts are right, and our ends prudently designed and ordered.

When our intentions are thus balanced, regulated, and discerned, we may consider, first that this exercise is of so universal efficacy that it is like the soul to every holy action, and must be provided for in every undertaking; and is of itself alone sufficient to make all natural and indifferent actions to be adopted into the family of religion. Secondly, that there are some actions which are usually reckoned as parts of our religion, which yet of themselves are so relative and imperfect, that without the purity of intention, they degenerate: and unless they be directed and proceed on to those purposes which God designed them to, they return into the family of common, secular, or sinful actions. Thus, alms are for charity, fasting for temperance, prayer is for religion, humiliation is for humility, austerity or sufferance is in order to the virtue of patience: and when these actions fail of their several ends, or are not directed to their own purposes, alms are misspent, fasting is an impertinent trouble, prayer is but lip-labour, humiliation is but hypocrisy, sufferance is but vexation; for such were the alms of the Pharisee, the fast of Jezebel, the prayer of Judah (reproved by the prophet Isaiah), the humiliation of Ahab, the martyrdom of heretics; in which nothing is given to God but the body, or the forms of religion. The soul and the power of godliness is wholly wanting. Thirdly, we are to consider that no intention can sanctify an unholy or unlawful action. Saul, the pharisee, persecuted the church of God with a design to do God service: and they that killed the apostles had also good purposes, but they had unhallowed actions. When there is both truth in election, and charity in the intention; when we go to God in ways of his own choosing or approving, then our eye is single, and our hands are clean, and our hearts are pure. But when a man does evil that good may come of it, or good to an evil purpose, that man does like him that rolls himself in thorns that he may sleep easily; he roasts himself in the fire that he may quench his thirst with his own sweat; he turns his face to the east that he may go to bed with the sun. I end this with the saying of a wise heathen: 'He is to be called evil that is good only for his own sake. Regard not how full hands you bring to God, but how pure. Many cease from sin out of fear alone, not out of innocence or love of virtue, and they, as yet, are not to be called innocent but timorous'.

A prayer for holy intention in the beginning and pursuit of any considerable action, as study, preaching etc.
O eternal God, who has made all things for man, and man for Thy glory, sanctify my body and soul, my thoughts and my intentions, my words and actions, that whatsoever I shall think, or speak, or do, may be to the glorification of Thy name; and by Thy blessing be effective and successful. Lord, turn my necessities into virtue; the works of nature into the works of grace, by making them orderly, regular, temperate, subordinate, and profitable to ends beyond their own. Let no pride or self-seeking, no covetousness or revenge, no impure mixture or unhandsome purposes, no little ends and low imaginations pollute my spirit, and unhallow any of my words and actions; but let my body be a servant of my spirit, and both body and spirit servants of Jesus.

III THE PRACTICE OF THE PRESENCE OF GOD

That God is present in all places, that He sees every action, hears all discourses, and understands every thought, is no strange thing to a Christian ear. 'For in Him we live, and move, and have our being'.[6] God is wholly in every place, included in no place; not bound with cords except those of love; not divided into parts, not changeable into several shapes; filling heaven and earth with His present power and with His never absent nature; and we can no more be removed from the presence of God than from our own being.

Several manners of the Divine Presence

1. God is present by His essence; which, because it is infinite, cannot be contained within the limits of any place; and as the sun, reflecting upon the mud of strands and shores, is unpolluted in its beams, so is God not dishonoured when we suppose Him in every one of His creatures, and in every part of every one of them; and is still as unmixed with any unhandsome adherence, as is the soul in the bowels of the body.

2. God is everywhere present by His power. He rolls the orbs of heaven with His hand; He fixes the earth with His foot; He guides all the creatures with His eye, and refreshes them with His influence: He makes the powers of hell to shake with His terrors, and binds the devils with His word, and throws them out with His command: and sends the angels on embassies with His decrees: He hardens the joints of infants, and makes firm the bones, when they are fashioned beneath secretly in the earth.

3. God is more specially present, by the several manifestations of Himself to extraordinary purposes. First, by glory, that is walking with God, dwelling or being with Him. 'I desire to be dissolved and to be with Christ': so said St. Paul. But this manner of Divine Presence is reserved for the elect people of God, and for their portion in their country.

4. God is, by grace and benediction, specially present in holy places, and in the solemn assemblies of His servants.⁷ If holy people meet in grots and dens of the earth, when persecution or a public necessity disturbs the public order, God fails not to come thither to them: but God is also, by the same or a greater reason, present there where they meet ordinarily, by order, and public authority. God will go out of His way to meet His saints and His presence signifies nothing but a readiness to hear their prayers, to bless their persons, to accept their offices, and to like even the circumstance of orderly and public meeting. God's love of order, and the reasonable customs of religion, have in ordinary, and in a certain degree, fixed this manner of His presence; and He loves to have it so.

5. God is especially present in the hearts of His people, by His Holy Spirit: and indeed the hearts of holy men are temples in the truth of things, and in type and shadow they are heaven itself. For God reigns in the hearts of His servants: there is His kingdom. The power of grace hath subdued all His enemies: there is His power. They serve Him night and day, and give Him thanks and praise; that is His glory. The temple itself is the heart of man; God dwells in our heart by faith, and Christ by His Spirit, and the Spirit by His purities: so that we are also cabinets of the mysterious Trinity: and what is this short of heaven itself, but as infancy is short of manhood and letters of

words? The same state of life it is, but not the same age. It is heaven
in a looking-glass, dark, but yet true, representing the beauties of the
soul, and the graces of God, and the images of His eternal glory, by
the reality of a special presence.

6. God is especially present in the consciences of all persons, good
and bad, by way of testimony and judgment: He is a remembrancer to
call our actions to mind, a witness to bring them to judgment, and a
judge to acquit or to condemn. And although this manner of presence is, in this life, after the manner of this life, that is, imperfect, and
we forget many actions of our lives; yet the greatest changes of our
state of grace or sin, our most considerable actions, are always present
like capital letters to an aged and dim eye. Because we covered them
with dust and negligence, they were not then discerned. But when we
are risen from our dust and imperfection, they all appear plain and
legible.

Now the consideration of this great truth is of a very universal use
in the whole course of the life of a Christian. He that remembers that
God stands a witness and a judge, beholding every secrecy, besides his
impiety, must have put on impudence, if he be not much restrained
in his temptation to sin. He is to be feared in public, He is to be
feared in private. Be sure, that while you are in His sight, you behave
yourself as becomes so holy a presence. But if you will sin, retire
yourself wisely, and go where God cannot see for nowhere else can
you be safe. And certainly, if men would always actually consider
and really esteem this truth, that God is the great eye of the world,
always watching over our actions, and an ever-open ear to hear all
our words, it would be the readiest way in the world to make sin to
cease from amongst the children of men, and for men to approach
to the blessed estate of the saints in heaven, who cannot sin, for
they always walk in the presence, and behold the face of God.

This is to be reduced to practice, according to the following
rules:

Rules of exercising this consideration
1. Let this actual thought often return, that God is omnipresent, filling every place; and say with David, 'Whither shall I go from Thy

Spirit, or whither shall I flee from Thy presence? If I ascend up into heaven, Thou art there; if I make my bed in hell, Thou art there'.[8]

2. In the beginning of actions of religion, make an act of adoration, that is, solemnly worship God, and place thyself in God's presence, and behold Him with the eye of faith; and let thy desires actually fix on Him, as the object of thy worship, and the reason of thy hope, and the fountain of thy blessing.

3. Let everything you see represent to your spirit the presence, the excellency, and the power of God; and let your conversation with the creatures lead you unto the Creator; for so shall your actions be done more frequently, with an actual eye to God's presence, by your often seeing Him in the glass of the creation. In the face of the sun you may see God's beauty; in the fire you may feel His heat warming; in the water His gentleness to refresh you: He it is that comforts your spirit when you have taken cordials; it is the dew of heaven that makes your field give you bread. This philosophy, which is obvious to every man's experience, is a good advantage to our piety; and, by this act of understanding, our wills are checked from violence and misdemeanour.

4. In your retirement, make frequent colloquies, between God and your own soul. 'Seven times a day do I praise Thee; and in the night season also I thought upon Thee, while I was waking'. So did David; and every act of complaint or thanksgiving, every act of rejoicing or of mourning, and every petition is a going to God, an appearing in His presence, and a building to God a chapel in our heart. It reconciles Martha's employment with Mary's devotion, charity and religion, the necessities of our calling, and the employments of devotion. For thus, in the midst of the works of your trade, you may retire into your chapel, your heart; and converse with God.

5. Represent and offer to God acts of love and fear. For, as God is everywhere present by His power, He calls for reverence and godly fear: as He is present to thee in all thy needs, and relieves them, He deserves thy love: and since, in every accident of our lives, we find one or other of these apparent, and in most things we see both, it is proper that, in every such demonstration of God, we ever obey Him because we love Him, and because we fear to offend Him. This is that which Enoch did who thus 'walked with God'.

6. Let us remember that God is in us, and that we are in Him: we are His workmanship, let us not deface it; we are in His presence, let us not pollute it by unholy and impure actions.

7. God is in the bowels of thy brother; refresh them when he needs it, and then you give your alms in the presence of God, and to God; and He feels the relief, which thou providest for thy brother.

8. God is in every place: suppose it therefore to be a church; and that decency of deportment and piety of carriage which you are taught by religion, or by custom, or by civility and public manners, to use in churches, the same use in all places.

9. God is in every creature; be cruel towards none, neither abuse any by intemperance.

10. He walks as in the presence of God that converses with Him in frequent prayer and frequent communion; in all his necessities, in all doubtings; that opens all his wants to Him; that weeps before Him for his sins; that asks remedy and support for his weakness; that fears Him as a Judge; reverences Him as a Lord; obeys Him as a Father; and loves Him.

The benefits of this exercise

Considering the Divine presence is, First, an excellent help to prayer, and actual devotion in our offices. Secondly, it produces a confidence in God, and fearlessness of our enemies, patience in trouble, and hope of remedy. Since God is so nigh in all our sad accidents especially, by promise, with us in tribulation, our greatest trouble may entitle us to a new manner of the Divine presence. Thirdly, it produces joy and rejoicing in God. We are of the same household with Him; He is with us in our natural actions, to preserve us; in our recreations, to restrain us; in our public actions, to applaud or reprove us; in our private, to observe us; in our sleeps, to watch by us; in our watchings, to refresh us: and if we walk with God in all His ways, as He walks with us in all ours, we shall 'Rejoice in the Lord always, and again I say rejoice'. And this puts me in mind of a saying of St. Anthony,—'There is one way of overcoming our ghostly enemies; spiritual mirth, and a perpetual bearing of God in our minds'. Fourthly, it produces joy, when we do enjoy Him; the same desires that a weak man hath for a defender; the sick man, for a physician; the child, for his father; the espoused lover, for her betrothed. Fifthly, humility of spirit. It is the cause of great modesty and decency in our actions; it helps to recollection of mind, and restrains the scatterings and looseness of wandering thoughts; it establishes the heart in good purposes, and leadeth on to perseverance; it gains purity and perfection (according to the saying of God to Abraham, 'walk before me and be perfect'), holy fear, and holy love, and indeed everything that pertains to holy living.

A Prayer meditating the Divine Presence

This Prayer is especially to be used in temptation to private sin.
O Almighty God, infinite and eternal, Thou art in the consciences of all men. Teach me to walk always as in Thy presence, to fear Thy majesty, to reverence Thy wisdom: that I may never dare to commit any indecency in the eye of my Lord and my Judge; that I, expressing the belief of Thy presence here, may feel the effects of it in eternal glory; through Jesus Christ. Amen.

Prayers and devotions, founded on the foregoing considerations

For Grace to spend our time well

O Eternal God, give me grace that I may be a careful and prudent spender of my time, so as best to prevent or resist all temptation, and be profitable to the Christian commonwealth. Take from me all slothfulness, and give me a diligent and an active spirit, and wisdom to choose my employment and fill up all the spaces of my time with actions of religion and charity; that, when the devil assaults me, he may not find me idle; for my dearest Saviour's sake. Amen.

For the Church

Let Thy mercy descend upon the whole Church; preserve her in truth and peace, in unity and safety, in all storms and against all temptations and enemies; that she, offering to Thy glory the never-ceasing sacrifice of prayer and thanksgiving, may advance the honour of her Lord, and be filled with His Spirit, and partake of His glory. Amen.

For the Sovereign
In mercy, remember the King (or Queen) ; preserve his person in health and honour ;
his crown in wealth and dignity ; his kingdoms in peace and plenty ; the churches
under his protection in piety and knowledge, and a strict and holy religion : keep him
perpetually in thy fear and favour, and crown him with glory and immortality. Amen.

For the Clergy
Remember them that minister about holy things ; let them be clothed with righteousness, and sing with joyfulness. Amen.

For wife or husband
Bless Thy servant (my wife, or husband) with health of body and of spirit. Let the
hand of Thy blessing be upon his head, night and day, and support him in all
necessities, strengthen him in all temptations, comfort him in all his sorrows, and let
him be Thy servant in all changes ; and make us both to dwell with Thee for ever in
Thy favour, in the light of Thy countenance, and in Thy glory. Amen.

For our children
Bless my children with healthful bodies, with good understandings, with the graces
and gifts of Thy Spirit, with sweet dispositions and holy habits ; and sanctify them
throughout in their bodies, and souls, and spirits, and keep them unblameable to the
coming of the Lord Jesus. Amen.

For friends and benefactors
Be pleased, O Lord, to remember my friends, all that have prayed for me, and all
that have done me good. (Here name those whom you would especially recommend).
Do Thou good to them, and return all their kindness double into their own bosom,
rewarding them with blessings, and sanctifying them with Thy graces, and bringing
them to glory. Amen

For all in misery
Relieve and comfort all the persecuted and afflicted ; speak peace to troubled consciences :
strengthen the weak, confirm the strong : instruct the ignorant : deliver the oppressed
from him that spoileth him, and relieve the needy that hath no helper : and bring us
all by the waters of comfort, and in the ways of righteousness, to the kingdom of rest
and glory, through Jesus Christ, our Lord. Amen.

NOTES: CHAPTER I

1 Ezek. XVI[49]
2 Jer. XLVIII[10]
3 1 Cor. VII[5]
4 1 Cor. X[31]

5 See Chapter 1, Section 1 Rule 18
6 Acts XVII[28]
7 Matt. XVIII[20] Heb. X[25]
8 Psalm CXXXIX[7, 8]

2 · Christian sobriety

Christian religion, in all its moral parts, is nothing else but the law of nature, and great reason; complying with the necessities of all the world, promoting the profit of all relations, and carrying us, through all accidents of variety of chances, to that end which God hath from eternal ages purposed for all that live according to it, and which he hath revealed in Jesus Christ: and, according to the apostle's arithmetic, hath but these three parts of it: Sobriety, Justice, Religion. The first contains all our deportment in our personal and private capacities, the fair treating of our bodies and our spirits. The second enlarges our duty in all relations to our neighbour. The third contains the offices of direct religion, and entercourse with God.

Christian sobriety is all that duty that concerns ourselves in the matter of meat and drink and pleasures and thoughts; and it hath within it the duties of temperance, chastity, humility, modesty, and content.

It is a using severity, denial and frustration of our appetite, when it grows unreasonable in any of these instances: the necessity of which we shall to best purpose understand, by considering the evil consequences of sensuality, effeminacy, or fondness after carnal pleasures.

Evil consequences of voluptuousness or sensuality

1. A longing after sensual pleasures is a dissolution of the spirit of a man, and makes it loose, soft, and wandering; unfit for noble, wise, or spiritual employments; because the principles upon which pleasure is chosen and pursued are sottish, weak, and unlearned, such as prefer the body before the soul, the appetite before reason, sense before the spirit, the pleasures of a short abode before the pleasures of eternity.

2. The nature of sensual pleasure is vain, empty, and unsatisfying, biggest always in expectation, and a mere vanity in the enjoying. Our laughing, if it be loud and high, commonly ends in a deep sigh; and all such pleasures have a sting in the tail, though they carry beauty on the face and sweetness on the lip.

3. Sensual pleasure is a great abuse to the spirit of a man, being a kind of fascination or witchcraft, blinding the understanding and enslaving the will. And he that knows he is free-born, or redeemed with the blood of the Son of God, will not easily suffer the freedom of his soul to be entangled and rifled.

4. It is most contrary to the state of a Christian, whose life is a wrestling and a warfare, to which sensual pleasure disables him, by yielding to that enemy with whom he must strive if ever he will be crowned. And this argument the apostle intimated: he 'that striveth for masteries is temperate in all things; now they do it to obtain a corruptible crown, but we an incorruptible'.[1]

5. It is the greatest impediment in the world to martyrdom. A Christian must first have crucified the lesser affections: for he that is overcome by little arguments of pain, will hardly consent to lose his life with torments.

Degrees of sobriety

Against this voluptuousness, sobriety is opposed in three degrees.

1. A resolving against all entertainment of the instances and temptations of sensuality; and it consists in the internal faculties of will and understanding, declaring against them, disapproving and disliking them, upon good reason and strong resolution.

2. A fight against all the temptations and offers of sensual pleasure

in all evil instances; and it consists in prayer, in fasting, in cheap diet and hard lodging, and laborious exercises, fortifying the spirit, and making it severe, manly, and Christian.

3. Spiritual pleasure is the highest degree of sobriety; and in the same degree in which we relish and are in love with spiritual delights, with the sweetnesses of devotion, with the joys of thanksgiving, with rejoicing in the Lord, with the comforts of hope, with the delicious-ness of charity with the sweetness of a good conscience, with the peace of meekness, and the felicities of a contented spirit; in the same degree we loathe the husks of swinish lusts, and the parings of the apples of Sodom, and the taste of sinful pleasures is unsavoury as the drunkard's vomit.

Rules for suppressing voluptuousness

The precepts and advices which are of best and of general use in the curing of sensuality, are these:

1. Accustom thyself to cut off all superfluity in the provisions of thy life. We must more take care that our desires should cease than that they should be satisfied.

2. Suppress your sensual desires in their first approach; for then they are least, but if they, in their weakness, prevail upon thy strengths, there will be no resisting them when they are increased. You shall scarce obtain of them to end, if you suffer them to begin.

3. Divert them with some laudable employment, and take off their edge by inadvertency, or a not-attending to them. For, since the facul-ties of a man cannot at the same time, with any sharpness, attend to two objects, if you employ your spirit upon a book or a bodily labour, or any innocent employment, you have no room left for the present trouble of a sensual temptation.

4. Look upon pleasures, not upon that side that is next the sun, or where they look beauteously; but when thou hast rifled and discom-posed them with enjoying their false beauties, and that they begin to go off, then behold them in their nakedness and weariness. Next time they counterfeit, remember what you have already discovered, and be no more abused. And I have known some wise persons have advised to cure the passions and longings of their children by letting

them taste of everything they passionately fancied; for they should be sure to find less in it than they looked for, and the impatience of their being denied would be loosened and made slack. The vanity of the possession will soon reprove the violence of the appetite. And if this permission be in innocent cases it may be of good use: but Solomon tried it in all things, taking his fill of all pleasures, and soon grew weary of them all. The same thing we may do by reason which we do by experience, if either we will look upon pleasures as we are sure they look when they go off, after their enjoyment; or if we will credit the experience of those men who have tasted them and loathed them.

5. Often consider and contemplate the joys of heaven, that when they have filled thy desires, which are the sails of the soul, thou mayest steer only thither, and never more look back to Sodom. And when thy soul dwells above, the pleasures of the world seem like things at distance, little and contemptible; and men running after the satisfaction of their sottish appetites seem foolish as fishes, thousands of them running after a rotten worm, that covers a deadly hook; or at best but like children, with great noise pursuing a bubble rising from a walnut shell, which ends sooner than the noise.

6. To this, the example of Christ will much help; who, understanding how to distinguish good from evil, did choose a sad and melancholy way to felicity, rather than the broad, pleasant, and easy path to folly and misery. But this is but the general principle. Its first particular is temperance.

II TEMPERANCE IN EATING AND DRINKING

Sobriety is the bridle of the passions of desire, and temperance is the bit and curb of that bridle, a restraint put into a man's mouth, a moderate use of meat and drink, so as may best consist with our health, and may not hinder but help the works of the soul by ministering cheerfulness and refreshment.

Temperance is a grace that chooses natural means in order to proper, and natural, and holy ends. It is exercised about eating and drinking, because they are necessary; but only as they minister to lawful ends : it does not eat and drink for pleasure, but for need, and for refreshment, which is a part or a degree of need. I deny not that eating and drinking may be, and in healthful bodies always are, with pleasure; because there is in nature no greater pleasure than that all the appetites which God hath made should be satisfied; and a man may choose a morsel that is pleasant (the less pleasant being rejected as being less useful, less apt to nourish) or more agreeing with an infirm stomach, or when the day is festival by order, or by private joy. The chief reason why we choose the more delicious is the serving that end for which such refreshments and choices are permitted. But when delight is the only end, then eating and drinking is an inordinate action; because it is not in the way to that end whither God directed it. But the choosing of a delicate before a more ordinary dish is to be done as other human actions are, in which there are no degrees and precise natural limits described, but a latitude is indulged; it must be done moderately, prudently, and God, who gave us such variety of creatures, and our choice to use which we will, may receive glory from our temperate use, and thanksgiving.

But temperance in meat and drink is to estimated by the following measures :

Measures of temperance in eating

1. Eat not before the time, unless necessity, or charity, or any intervening accident, which may make it reasonable and prudent, should happen. Remember, it had almost cost Jonathan his life, because he tasted a little honey before the sun went down, contrary to the king's commandment; and although a great need which he had, excused him from the sin of gluttony, yet it is inexcusable when thou eatest before the usual time, and thrustest thy hand into the dish unseasonably, out of greediness of the pleasure, and impatience of the delay.

2. Eat not hastily and impatiently, but with such decent and timely action that your eating be a human act, subject to deliberation and choice. He that eats hastily may contract many little undecencies, and be suddenly surprised.

3. Be not troublesome to thyself or others in the choice of thy

meats or the delicacy of thy sauces. It is lawful in all senses to comply with a weak and a nice stomach: but not with a nice and curious palate. When our health requires it, that ought to be provided for; but not so our sensuality and intemperate longings. Whatsoever is set before you eat; if it be provided for you, you may eat it, be it never so delicate; and be it plain and common, so it be wholesome and fit for you, it must not be refused. Moderation is to be reckoned in proportion to the present customs, to the company, to education, to the judgment of honest and wise persons, and the necessities of nature.

4. Eat not too much: load neither thy stomach nor thy understanding. 'If thou sit at a bountiful table, be not greedy upon it, and say not there is much meat on it. Remember that a wicked eye is an evil thing: and what is created more wicked than an eye? Therefore it weepeth upon every occasion. A very little is sufficient for a man well nurtured'.[2]

Signs and effects of temperance
We shall best know that we have the grace of temperance by the following signs, which are so many arguments to engage us also upon its study and practice.

A temperate man is modest: greediness is unmannerly and rude. Temperance is accompanied with gravity of deportment: greediness is garish. Sound but moderate sleep is its sign and its effect. 'Sound sleep cometh of moderate eating; he riseth early, and his wits are with him'.[3] A spiritual joy and a devout prayer. A suppressed and seldom anger. A command of our thoughts and passions. A seldom-returning and a never-prevailing temptation. To which add, that a temperate person thinks not much, and speaks not often, of meat and drink; hath a healthful body and long life, unless it be hindered by some other accident: whereas to gluttony, the pain of watching and choler, the pangs of the belly, are continual company.

Of drunkenness
Because intemperance in eating is not so soon perceived by others as immoderate drinking, and the outward visible effects of it are not either so notorious or so ridiculous, therefore gluttony is not of so

great disreputation amongst men as drunkenness. Gluttony is more uncharitable to the body, and drunkenness to the soul, or the understanding part of man; and therefore in Scripture is more frequently forbidden and declaimed against than the others.

Drunkenness is an immoderate affection and use of drink. That I call immoderate, that is besides or beyond that order of good things for which God hath given us the use of drink. The ends are, digestion of our meat, cheerfulness and refreshment of our spirits, or any end of health. If at any time we go beyond, it is inordinate—it is the vice of drunkenness. It is forbidden by our blessed Saviour in these words: 'Take heed to yourselves, lest at any time your hearts be overcharged with surfeiting and drunkenness'.[4] For Christ forbids both the actual and the habitual intemperance; not only the effect of it, but also the affection to it: for in both there is sin. It is a sin not to prevent such uncharitable effects upon the body and understanding; and therefore a man that loves not the drink is guilty of surfeiting, if he does not watch to prevent the evil effect: and it is a sin, and the greater of the two, inordinately to love or to use the drink, though the surfeiting or violence do not follow. Good therefore is the counsel of the son of Sirach, 'Show not thy valiantness in wine; for wine hath destroyed many'.[5]

Evil consequences of drunkenness

It causeth woes and mischief,[6] wounds and sorrow, sin and shame; it maketh bitterness of spirit, brawling and quarrelling; it increaseth rage and lesseneth strength; it maketh red eyes, and a loose and babbling tongue. It particularly ministers to lust, and yet disables the body; so that in effect it makes man wanton as a satyr, and impotent as age. And Solomon, adds this to the account 'Thine eyes shall behold strange women, and thine heart shall utter perverse things',[7] as if the drunkard were only desire, and then impatience, muttering and enjoying like an eunuch embracing a woman. It besots and hinders the actions of the understanding, making a man brutish in his passions, and a fool in his reason; and differs nothing from madness, but that it is voluntary, and so is an equal evil in nature, and a worse in manners. It takes off all the guards, and lets ℓoose the reins of all those evils to which a man is by his nature or by his evil customs inclined, and from which he is restrained by reason and principles. Drunkenness calls off the watchmen from their towers; and then all the evils that can, proceed from a loose heart, and an untied tongue, and a dissolute spirit, and an unguarded, unlimited will. It extinguisheth and quenches the Spirit of God; for no man can be filled with the Spirit of God and with wine at the same time. And therefore St. Paul makes them exclusive of each other: 'Be not drunk with wine, wherein is excess, but be filled with the Spirit'.[8] And since Joseph's cup was put into Benjamin's sack, no man hath a divining goblet. It opens all the sanctuaries of nature, and discovers the nakedness of the soul, all its weaknesses and follies; it multiplies sins and discovers them; it makes a man incapable of being a private friend or a public counsellor. It taketh a man's soul into slavery and imprisonment more than any vice whatsoever,[9] because it disarms a man of all his reason and his wisdom, whereby he might be cured; and commonly it grows upon him with age, a drunkard being still more a fool and less a man. I need not add any sad examples, since all story and all ages have too many of them. Amnon was slain by his brother Absalom when he was warm and high with wine. Simon, the high priest, and two of his sons, were slain by their brother at a drunken feast. Holofernes was drunk when Judith slew him: and all the great things that Daniel spake of Alexander were drowned with a surfeit of one night's intemperance.

Signs of drunkenness

Drunkenness is in the same manner to be judged as sickness. As every illness or violence done to health, in every part of its continuance is a part or degree of sickness: so is every going off from our natural and common temper and our usual severity of behaviour, a degree of drunkenness. Its parts and periods are usually thus reckoned: apish gestures; much talking; immoderate laughing; dullness of sense; scurrility, that is, wanton, or jeering, or abusive language; a useless understanding; stupid sleep; fallings and reelings, and beastly vomitings. The least of these, even when the tongue begins to be untied, is a degree of drunkenness.

Rules for obtaining temperance

1. Be not often present at feasts, nor at all in dissolute company, when it may be avoided. But if you be unavoidably or indiscreetly engaged, let not mistaken civility or good nature engage thee either to the temptation of staying (if thou understandest thy weakness), or the sin of drinking inordinately.

2. Be severe in your judgment concerning your proportions, and let no occasion make you enlarge far beyond your ordinary. But remember this, whenever you begin to consider whether you may safely take one draught more, it is then high time to give over.

3. Come not to table but when thy need invites thee: and if thou beest in health, leave something of thy appetite unfilled, something of thy natural heat unemployed, that it may secure thy digestion, and serve other needs of nature or the spirit.

4. Propound to thyself (if thou beest in a capacity) a constant rule of living, of eating and drinking: which though it may not be fit to observe scrupulously, lest it become a snare to thy conscience, or endanger thy health upon every accidental violence; yet let not thy rule be broken often nor much, but upon great necessity and in small degrees.

5. Never urge any man to eat or drink beyond his own limits and his own desires.

6. Use St. Paul's instruments of sobriety: 'Let us who are of the day be sober, putting on the breastplate of faith and love, and, for an helmet, the hope of salvation',[10] Faith, hope, and charity are the best weapons in the world to fight against intemperance. The faith of the Mahometans forbids them to drink wine, and they abstain religiously, as the sons of Rechab. The faith of Christ forbids drunkenness to us; and therefore is infinitely more powerful to suppress this vice, when we remember that we are Christians, and to abstain from drunkenness and gluttony is part of the faith and discipline of Jesus; and that with with these vices neither our love to God, nor our hopes of heaven, can possibly consist.

7. As a pursuance of this rule, it is a good advice, that we begin and end all our times of eating with prayer and thanksgiving.

8. Mingle discourses, pious, or in some sense profitable, and in all

senses charitable and innocent, with thy meal, as occasion is ministered.

9. Let your drink so serve your meat as your meat doth your health; that it be apt to convey and digest it, and refresh the spirits: but let it never go beyond such a refreshment as may a little lighten the present load of a sad or troubled spirit.

10. Be careful that you be not brought under the power of such things, which otherwise are lawful enough in use. 'All things are lawful for me; but I will not be brought under the power of any', saith St. Paul. And to be perpetually longing, and impatiently desirous of anything, so that a man cannot abstain from it, is to lose a man's liberty, and to become a servant of meat and drink, or smoke. And I wish this last instance were more considered by persons who little suspect themselves guilty of intemperance, though their desires are strong and impatient, and the use of it perpetual, and unreasonable to all purposes but that they have made it habitual and necessary, as intemperance itself is made to some men.

11. Use those advices which are prescribed as means for suppressing voluptuousness in the foregoing section.

III CHASTITY

An introductory warning, to be read before going on further

Reader, stay, and read not the advices of the following section, unless thou hast a chaste spirit; or desirest to be chaste; or at least art apt to consider, whether you ought or no. For there are some so wholly possessed with a spirit of uncleanness, that they turn the most prudent and chaste discourses into dirt and filthy apprehensions; and in a literal sense turning the grace of God into wantonness. They study cases of conscience in the matter of carnal sins, not to avoid, but to learn ways to pollute their spirits: and search their houses with a sunbeam, that they may be instructed in all the corners of nastiness. If any man will snatch the pure taper from my hand and hold it to the devil, he will only burn his own fingers, but shall not rob me of the reward of my care and good intention, since I have taken heed how to express the following duties, and given him caution how to read them.

Chastity is a suppression of all irregular desires in the matters of sensual or carnal pleasure. I call all desires irregular and sinful that are not sanctified : by the holy institution, or by being within the protection of marriage; by being within the order of nature; or by being within the moderation of Christian modesty. Against the first are fornication, adultery, and all voluntary pollutions of either sex : against the second are all unnatural lusts and incestuous mixtures : against the third is all immoderate use of permitted beds; concerning which judgment is to be made, as concerning meats and drinks : there being no certain degree of frequency or intention prescribed to all persons; but it is to be ruled as the other actions of a man, by proportion to the end, and by the dignity of the person in the honour and severity of being a Christian.

Chastity is that grace which forbids and restrains all these, keeping the body and soul pure. Our duty is thus described by St. Paul : 'For this is the will of God, even your sanctification, that ye should abstain from fornication : that every one of you should know how to possess his vessel in sanctification and honour; not in the lust of concupiscence, even as the Gentiles which know not God'.[11]

Chastity is either abstinence or continence. Abstinence is that of virgins or widows; continence belongs to married persons. Chaste marriages are honourable and pleasing to God; widowhood is pitiable in its solitariness and loss, but amiable and comely when it is adorned with gravity and purity, and not sullied with remembrances of the past licence, nor with present desires of returning to a second bed. But virginity is a life of angels, the enamel of the soul, the huge advantage of religion, the great opportunity for the retirements of devotions; and, being empty of cares, it is full of prayers; being unmingled with the world, it is apt to converse with God.

Natural virginity of itself is not a state more acceptable to God : but that which is chosen and voluntary, in order to the conveniences of religion and separation from worldly encumbrances, is therefore better than the married life, not that it is more holy, but that it is a freedom from cares, an opportunity to spend more time in spiritual employments.

But some married persons, even in their marriage, do better please

God than some virgins in their state of virginity : they, by giving
great example of conjugal affection, by preserving their faith un-
broken, by educating children in the fear of God, by patience and
contentedness, and holy thoughts, and the exercise of virtues proper
to that state, do not only please God, but do so in a higher degree
than those virgins whose piety is not answerable to their great
opportunities and advantages.

The evil consequences of uncleanness

The blessings and proper effects of chastity we shall best understand,
by reckoning up the evils of uncleanness and carnality.

1. Uncleanness, of all vices, is the most shameful. 'The eye also of
the adulterer waiteth for the twilight, saying, No eye shall see me ;
and disguiseth his face'.[12] Shame is the eldest daughter of uncleanness.

2. The appetites of uncleanness are full of cares and trouble, and its
fruition is sorrow and repentance. The way of the adulterer is hedged
with thorns ;[13] full of fears and jealousies, burning desires and
impatient waitings, tediousness of delay, and sufferance of affronts,
and amazements of discovery.

3. Most of its kinds are of that condition that they involve the
ruin of two souls, and he that is a fornicator or adulterous, steals the
soul, as well as dishonours the body, of his neighbour ; and so it
becomes like the sin of falling Lucifer, who brought a part of the
stars with himself from heaven.

4. Of all carnal sins, it is that alone which the devil takes delight to
imitate and counterfeit, communicating with witches and impure
persons in the corporal act, but in this only.

5. Uncleanness is a vice which hath a professed enmity against
the body. 'He that committeth fornication sinneth against his own
body'.[14]

6. Uncleanness is hugely contrary to the spirit of government by
embasing the spirit of a man, making it sneaking soft and foolish,
without courage, without confidence. David felt this after his folly
with Bathsheba ; he fell to unkingly arts and stratagems to hide the
crime ; and he did nothing but increase it, and remained timorous and

poor spirited, till he prayed to God once more to establish him with a free and princely spirit.[15]

7. The Gospel hath added two arguments against uncleanness. Our bodies are made temples of the Holy Ghost, in which He dwells; and therefore uncleanness is sacrilege, and defiles a temple. It is St. Paul's argument, 'Know ye not that your body is the temple of the Holy Ghost?'[16] and 'He that defiles a temple, him will God destroy'. 'Therefore glorify God in your bodies';[17] that is, flee fornication.

8. The next special argument which the Gospel ministers is that marriage is by Christ hallowed into a mystery, to signify the sacramental and mystical union of Christ and His church.[18] He, therefore, that breaks this knot, which the church and their mutual faith hath tied, and Christ hath knit up into a mystery, dishonours a great rite of Christianity, of high, spiritual, and excellent signification.

9. St. Gregory reckons uncleanness to be the parent of these monsters; blindness of mind, inconsideration, precipitancy, or giddiness in actions, self-love, hatred of God, love of the present pleasures, a despite or despair of the joys of religion here, and of heaven hereafter. Whereas a pure mind in a chaste body is the mother of wisdom and deliberation, sober counsels and ingenuous actions, open deportment and sweet carriage, sincere principles and unprejudiced understanding, love of God and self-denial, peace and confidence, holy prayers and spiritual comfort, and a pleasure of spirit infinitely greater than the sottish and beastly pleasures of unchastity.

10. Add to all these, the public dishonesty and disreputation that all the nations of the world have cast upon adulterous and unhallowed embraces. The Egyptian law was to cut off the nose of the adulteress, and the offending part of the adulterer. The Locrians put out both the adulterer's eyes. The Germans (as Tacitus reports) placed the adulteress amidst her kindred naked, and shaved her head, and caused her husband to beat her with clubs through the city. The Cumani caused the woman to ride upon an ass, naked and hooted at, and for ever after called her by an appellation of scorn, 'a rider upon the ass'. All nations barbarous and civil agreeing in their general design, of rooting so dishonest and shameful a vice from under heaven.

The middle ages of the Church were not pleased that the adulteress should be put to death: but in the primitive ages, the civil laws by which Christians were then governed gave leave to the wronged husband to kill his adulterous wife if he took her in the fact.

Whether is worse, the adultery of the man or the woman? First, in respect of the person, the fault is greater in a man than in a woman, who is of a more passive nature and hath the armour of modesty, which is the natural ornament of that sex. 'It is unjust that the man should demand chastity and severity from his wife which himself will not observe towards her', said the good Emperor Antoninus: it is as if the man should persuade his wife to fight against those enemies to which he had yielded himself a prisoner. Secondly, in respect of the effects and evil consequences, the adultery of the woman is worse, so bringing bastardy into a family, and a great injuries to the lawful children, and infinite violations of peace, and divorces, and all the effects of rage and madness. Thirdly, as relating to God, they are equal, intolerable, and damnable; and the Church anciently refused to admit such persons to the holy communion, until they had done seven year's penances in fasting, in sackcloth, in severe inflictions and instruments of charity and sorrow, according to the discipline of those ages.

Acts of chastity in general
The actions of the grace of chastity are these:

1. To resist all unchaste thoughts; although no definite desire or resolution be entertained.

2. At no hand to entertain any desire, or any fanciful imaginative loves, though by shame, or disability, or other circumstance, they be restrained from act.

3. To have a chaste eye and hand: for it is all one with what part of the body we commit adultery, and if a man lets his eye loose and enjoys the lust of that, he is an adulterer. 'Look not upon a woman to lust after her'.

4. To have a heart and mind chaste and pure, that is, detesting all uncleanness; disliking all its motions, past actions, circumstances, likenesses, discourses: and this ought to be the chastity of virgins,

widows, and old persons especially, and generally of all men, according to their several necessities.

5. To discourse chastely and purely; declining all indecencies of language, chastening the tongue and restraining it with grace.

6. To disapprove by an after-act all involuntary and natural pollutions: for if a man delights in having suffered any such, and with pleasure remembers it, he chooses that which was in itself involuntary; and that which (being natural) was innocent, becoming voluntary, is made sinful.

7. They that have performed these duties and parts of chastity, will certainly abstain from all exterior actions of uncleanness, those noonday and midnight devils, whose birth is in trouble, whose growth is in folly, and whose end is in shame.

But besides these general acts of chastity which are common to all states of men and women, there are some few things proper to the severals.

Acts of virginal chastity

1. Virgins must remember, that the virginity of the body is only excellent in order to the purity of the soul; but else, it is no better than that of involuntary or constrained eunuchs; a misery and a trouble, or else a mere privation, as much without excellency as without mixture.

2. Virgins must contend for a singular modesty; pious and chaste thoughts, holy language, and modest carriage.

3. Looseness of society is a violence done to virginity, not in its natural, but in its moral capacity.

4. Virgins have a peculiar obligation to charity; for this is the virginity of the soul, as purity, integrity, and separation is of the body; which doctrine we are taught by St. Peter: 'Seeing ye have purified your souls in obeying the truth through the Spirit unto unfeigned love of the brethren, see that ye love one another with a pure heart fervently'.[19]

These rules are necessary for virgins that offer that state to God, and mean not to enter into the state of marriage; for they that only wait the opportunity of a convenient change, are to steer themselves by the general rules of chastity.

Rules for widows

For widows, the fontinel of whose desires hath been opened by the former permissions of the marriage-bed, they must remember,

1. That God hath now restrained the former licence, bound up their eyes and shut up their heart into a narrower compass, and hath given them sorrow to be a bridle to their desires. A widow must be a mourner; and she that is not cannot so well secure the chastity of her proper state.

2. It is against public honesty to marry another man, so long as she is with child by her former husband; and of the same fame, it is in a lesser proportion to marry within the year of mourning; but anciently it was infamous for her to marry till by common account the body was dissolved into its first principle of earth.

3. A widow must restrain her memory and her fancy, not recalling or recounting her former permissions and freer licences with any present delight; for then she opens that sluice which her husband's death and her own sorrow have shut up.

4. A widow that desires her widowhood should be a state pleasing to God, must spend her time as devoted virgins should, in fastings and prayers, and charity.

5. A widow must forbid herself to use those temporal solaces, which in her former estate were innocent, but now are dangerous.

Rules for married persons, or matrimonial chastity

Concerning married persons, besides the keeping of their mutual faith and contract with each other, these particulars are useful to be observed.

1. Although their mutual endearments are safe within the protection of marriage, they must have an affection greater to each other than they have to any person in the world, but not greater than they have to God: but that they be ready to part with all interest in each other's person rather than sin against God.

2. In their permissions and licence, they must be sure to observe the order of nature, and the ends of God. He is an ill husband that uses his wife as a man treats a harlot, having no other end but pleasure. Concerning which our best rule is, that although in this,

as in eating and drinking, there is an appetite to be satisfied which
cannot be done without pleasing that desire; yet, since that desire
and satisfaction was intended by nature for other ends, they should
never be separate from those ends, but always be joined with all or
one of these ends, with a desire of children, or to avoid fornication,
or to lighten and ease the cares and sadnesses of household affairs,
or to endear each other: but never with a purpose, either in act or
desire, to separate the sensuality from these ends which hallow it.

3. Married persons must keep such modesty and decency of treating each other, that they never force themselves into high and violent
lusts, with arts and misbecoming devices; always remembering, that
those mixtures are most innocent which are most simple and most
natural, most orderly and most safe.

4. It is a duty of matrimonial chastity to be restrained and temperate in the use of their lawful pleasures. Married persons are to estimate
the degree of their licence according to the following proportions:
that it be moderate, so as to consist with health; that it be so ordered
as not to be too expensive of time, that precious opportunity of
working out our salvation; that when duty is demanded, it be always
paid (so far as is in our powers and election); and that it be with a
temperate affection, without violent transporting desires, or too
sensual applications. Concerning which a man is to make judgment
by proportion to other actions, always remembering that marriage is
a provision for supply of the natural necessities of the body, not for
the artificial and procured appetites of the mind. And it is a sad truth,
that many married persons, thinking that the floodgates of liberty are
set wide open without measure or restraints (so they sail in that
channel), have felt the final rewards of intemperance and lust, by their
unlawful using of lawful permissions. Only let each of them be
temperate, and both of them be modest. Socrates was wont to say
that those women to whom nature hath not been indulgent in good
features and colours, should make it up themselves with excellent
manners; and those who were beautiful and comely, should be careful
that so fair a body be not polluted with unhandsome usages. To
which Plutarch adds, that a wife, if she be unhandsome, should consider how extremely ugly she would be, if she wanted modesty; but

if she be handsome, let her think how gracious that beauty would be if she superadds chastity.

5. Married persons are to abstain by consent from their mutual entertainments at solemn times of devotion; not as a duty of itself necessary, but as being the most proper act of purity, which, in their condition, they can present to God. It is St. Paul's counsel, that 'by consent for a time they should abstain, that they may give themselves to fasting and prayer'.[20] And though when Christians did receive the holy communion every day, it is certain they did not abstain, but had children; yet, when the communion was more seldom, they did with religion abstain from the marriage-bed during the time of their solemn preparatory devotions, as anciently they did from eating and drinking, till the solemnity of the day was past.

6. It were well if married persons would, in their general confessions, suspect themselves, and accordingly ask a general pardon for all their undecencies, and more passionate applications of themselves in the the offices of marriage: that what is lawful and honourable in its kind may not be sullied with imperfect circumstances.

But because of all the dangers of a Christian none are more pressing and troublesome than the temptations to lust, no enemy more dangerous than that of the flesh, therefore it concerns all that would be safe from this death to arm themselves by the following rules, to prevent or to cure all the wounds of our flesh made by the poisoned arrows of lust.

Remedies against uncleanness

1. When a temptation of lust assaults thee, do not resist it by heaping up arguments against it, and disputing with it, but fly from it, that is, think not at all of it; lay aside all consideration concerning it, and turn away from it by any severe and laudable thought of business. Jerome very wittily reproves the gentile superstition, which pictured the virgin-deities armed with a shield and lance, as if chastity could not be defended without war and direct contention. No; this enemy is to be treated otherwise. If you listen to it, though but to dispute with it, it ruins you; and the very arguments you go about to answer, leave a relish upon the tongue.

2. Avoid idleness, and fill up all the spaces of thy time with severe and useful employment; for lust usually creeps in at those emptinesses where the soul is unemployed, and the body is at ease; for no easy, healthful, and idle person was ever chaste, if he could be tempted. But of all employments bodily labour is most useful and of greatest benefit for driving away the devil.

3. Give no entertainment to the beginnings, the first motions and secret whispers of the spirit of impurity. For if you totally suppress it, it dies; if you permit the furnace to breathe its smoke and flame out at any vent, it will rage to the consumption of the whole.

4. Corporal mortification, and hard usages of our body, hath by all ages of the Church, been accounted a good instrument, and of some profit against the spirit of fornication. And this was St. Paul's remedy, 'I bring my body under'; he used some rudenesses towards it. But it was a great nobleness of chastity which St. Jerome reports of a son of the King of Nicomedia, who, being tempted upon flowers and a perfumed bed with a soft violence, but yet tied down to the temptation, and solicited with circumstances of Asian luxury by an impure courtesan, lest the easiness of his posture should abuse him, spit out his tongue into her face: to represent that no virtue hath cost the saints so much as this of chastity.

5. Fly from all occasions, temptations, loosenesses of company, undecent mixtures of wanton dancings, idle talk, private society with strange women, starings upon a beauteous face, amorous gestures, garish and wanton dressings, feasts and liberty, wine and strong drinks, which are made to persecute chastity. Ever remember that it is easier to die for chastity than to live with it.

6. He that will secure his chastity, must first cure his pride and his rage. For oftentimes lust is the punishment of a proud man, and the same intemperate heat that makes anger, does enkindle lust.

7. If thou beest assaulted with an unclean spirit, trust not thyself alone; but run forth into company whose reverence and modesty may suppress, or whose society may divert thy thoughts.

8. Use frequent and earnest prayers, for beside the blessings of prayer, a prayer against it is an unwillingness to act it; and so long as we heartily pray against it our desires are secured, and then this

devil hath no power. This was St. Paul's other remedy: 'For this cause I besought the Lord thrice'. And there is much reason and advantage in this, because the main thing to be rescued is a man's mind.

9. Bring in succour from consideration of the Divine presence, meditation of death, and the passions of Christ upon the cross.

10. These remedies are of universal efficacy in all cases extra-ordinary and violent; but in ordinary and common, the remedy which God hath provided, that is, honourable marriage, hath a natural efficacy, besides a virtue by Divine blessings, to cure the inconveniences which otherwise might afflict persons temperate and sober.

IV HUMILITY

Humility is the great ornament and jewel of Christian religion, where-by it is distinguished from all the wisdom of the world; it not having been taught by the wise men of the Gentiles, but first put into a discipline, and made part of a religion, by our Lord Jesus Christ, in the twin sisters of meekness and humility. 'Learn of me, for I am meek and humble; and ye shall find rest unto your souls'.

Arguments against pride
1. Our body is weak and impure, sending out more uncleannesses from its several sinks than could be endured, if they were not necessary and natural.

2. Our strength is inferior to that of many beasts, and our infirmi-ties so many that we are forced to dress and tend horses and asses, that they may help our needs, and relieve our wants.

3. Our beauty is in colour inferior to many flowers, and in pro-portion of parts it is no better than nothing; for even a dog hath parts as well proportioned and fitted to his purposes, and the designs of his nature, as we have; and when it is most florid and gay, three fits of an ague can change it into yellowness and leanness, and the hollowness and wrinkles of deformity.

4. Our learning is then best when it teaches most humility: but to be proud of learning is the greatest ignorance in the world. For our learning is so long in getting, and so very imperfect, that the greatest

clerk knows not the thousandth part of what he is ignorant; and knows so uncertainly what he seems to know, that except those things which concern his duty, and which God hath revealed to him, the most learned man hath nothing to be proud of.

5. He that is proud of riches is a fool. For if he be exalted above his neighbours because he hath more gold, how much inferior is he to a gold mine?

6. If a man exalted by reason of any excellence in his soul, he may please to remember that all souls are equal; and their differing operations are because their instrument is in better tune, their body is more healthful or better tempered: which is no more praise to him than it is that he was born in Italy.

7. He that is proud of his birth is proud of the blessings of others, not of himself; and when himself was born, it was indifferent to him whether his father were a king or a peasant, for he knew not anything nor chose anything: and most commonly it is true, that he that boasts of his ancestors, who were the founders and raisers of a noble family, doth confess that he hath in himself a less virtue and a less honour, and therefore that he is degenerated.

8. Whatsoever other difference there is between thee and thy neighbour, if it be bad, it is thine own, but thou hast no reason to boast of thy misery and shame: if it be good, thou hast received it from God.

9. Remember what thou wert before thou wert begotten; nothing: what wert thou for many years after? weakness. What in all thy life? A great sinner. What in all thy excellences? A mere debtor to God, to thy parents, to the earth, to all the creatures. But we may, if we please use the method of the Platonists who reduce all the causes and arguments for humility to these seven heads. The spirit of man is light and troublesome; his body is brutish and sickly; he is constant in his folly and error, and inconsistent in his manners and good purposes; his labours are vain, intricate, and endless; his fortune is changeable, but seldom pleasing, never perfect; his wisdom comes not till he be ready to die, that is, till he be past using it; his death is certain, always ready at the door, but never far off. Upon these meditations we shall see nothing more reasonable than to be humble, and nothing more foolish than to be proud.

Acts of humility

The grace of humility is exercised by these following rules:

1. Think not thyself better for any thing that happens to thee from without. For although thou mayest, by gifts bestowed upon thee, be better than another, as one horse is better than another, that is of more use to others; yet as thou art a man, thou hast nothing to commend thee to thyself but that only by which thou art a man, that is by what thou choosest and refusest.

2. Humility consists not in railing against thyself, or wearing mean clothes, or going softly and submissively, but in real evil or mean opinion of thyself. Believe thyself an unworthy person heartily, as thou believest thyself to be hungry, or poor, or sick, when thou art so.

3. If thou callest thyself fool, be not angry if another say so of thee. For if thou thinkest so truly, all men in the world desire other men to be of their opinion; and he is an hypocrite that accuses himself before others with an intent not to be believed.

4. Love to be concealed and little esteemed; be content to want praise, never being troubled when thou art slighted or undervalued; for thou canst not undervalue thyself, and if thou thinkest so meanly as there is reason, no contempt will seem unreasonable, and therefore it will be very tolerable.

5. Never be ashamed of thy birth, or thy parents, or thy trade, or thy present employment, for the meanness or poverty of any of them; but speak as readily and indifferently of meanness as of greatness. Primislaus, the first king of Bohemia, kept his country shoes always by him, to remember from whence he was raised; and Agathocles, by the furniture of his table, confessed that from a potter he was raised to be the king of Sicily.

6. Never speak anything directly tending to thy praise or glory; that is, with the purpose to be commended, and for no other end.

7. When thou hast said or done anything for which thou receivest praise or estimation, take it indifferently, and return it to God, reflecting upon Him as the giver of the gift, or the blesser of the action, or the aid of the design; and give God thanks for making thee an instrument of His glory, for the benefit of others.

8. Secure a good name by living virtuously and humbly; let others use it for their own advantage, let them speak of it if they please, but do not thou at all use it but as an instrument to do God glory, and thy neighbour more advantage.

9. Take no content in praise when it is offered thee: but let thy rejoicing in God's gift be allayed with fear, lest this good bring thee to evil.

10. Use no stratagems and devices to get praise. Some inquire into the faults of their own actions or discourses, on purpose to hear that it was well done or spoken, and without fault; others bring the matter into talk, or thrust themselves into company, till by drinking the waters of vanity they swell and burst.

11. Make no suppletories to thyself, when thou art disgraced or slighted, by pleasing thyself with supposing thou didst deserve praise, though they understood thee not, or enviously detracted from thee: neither do thou get to thyself a private theatre and flatterers, in whose vain noises and fantastic praises thou mayest keep up thine own good opinion of thyself.

12. Entertain no fancies of vanity and private whispers of this devil of pride. Some fantastic spirits will walk alone, and dream waking of greatnesses, of palaces, of excellent orations, full theatres, loud applauses, sudden advancement, great fortunes, and so will spend an hour with imaginative pleasure; nothing but fumes of pride, and significations of what their heart wishes. In this, although there is nothing of its own nature directly vicious, yet it is at no hand consisting with the safety and interests of humility.

13. Suffer others to be praised in thy presence, and entertain their good and glory with delight; but at no hand disparage them, and think not the advancement of thy brother is a lessening of thy worth.

14. Be content that he should be employed, and thou laid by as unprofitable; his sentence approved, thine rejected; he be preferred, and thou fixed in a low employment.

15. Never compare thyself with others, unless it be to advance them and to depress thyself. To which purpose, we must be sure, in some sense or other, to think ourselves the worst in every company where we come; one is more learned than I am, another is more

prudent, a third honourable, a fourth more chaste, or he is more charitable, or less proud. Though it be good always to think meanest of ourselves, yet it is not ever safe to speak it, because those circumstances which determine thy thoughts, are not known to others as to thyself. But if thou preservest thy thoughts and opinions of thyself truly humble, you may with more safety give God thanks in public for that good which cannot or ought not to be concealed.

16. Be not always ready to excuse every oversight, or indiscretion, or ill action; but if thou beest guilty of it, confess it plainly; for virtue scorns a lie for its cover. If thou beest not guilty, unless it be scandalous, be not over-earnest to remove it, but rather use it as an argument to chastise all greatness of fancy and opinion in thyself; and accustom thyself to bear reproof patiently and contentedly.

17. Give God thanks for every weakness, deformity, and imperfection, and accept it as an instrument to resist pride, and nurse humility.

18. Be sure never to praise thyself, or to dispraise any man else, unless God's glory or some holy end do hallow it.

19. Humility teaches us to submit ourselves and all our faculties to God, 'to believe all things, to do all things, to suffer all things', which His will enjoins us; to be content in every estate or change; to adore His goodness, to fear His greatness, to worship His eternal and infinite excellences, and to submit ourselves to all our superiors in all things according to godliness, and to be meek and gentle in our conversation towards others.

Now although, according to the nature of every grace, this begins as a gift, and is increased like a habit, that is, best by its own acts; yet there are certain other exercises and considerations, which are good helps and instruments for the procuring and increasing this grace, and the curing of pride.

Means and exercises for obtaining and increasing the grace of humility
1. Make confession of thy sins often to God; and remember that he whose life seems fair by reason that his faults are scattered at large distances in the several parts of his life, yet if all his errors and follies were articled against him, the man would seem vicious and miserable.

And possibly this exercise, really applied upon thy spirit, may be useful.

2. Remember that we usually disparage others upon slight grounds and little instances. Let us therefore, since we are so severe to others, consider whatsoever good any one can think or say of us.

3. When our neighbour is cried up by public fame and popular noises, we cry out that the people is a herd of unlearned and ignorant persons, ill judges, loud trumpets, but which never give certain sound; let us use the same art to humble ourselves, and never take delight and pleasure in public reports and acclamations of assemblies.

4. We change our opinion of others by their kindness or unkindness towards us. If he be my patron, and bounteous, he is wise, he is noble, his faults are but warts, his virtues are mountainous; but if he proves unkind, or rejects our importunate suit, then he is ill-natured, covetous, and his free meal is called gluttony. This indeed is unjust towards others, but a good instrument if we turn the edge of it upon ourselves. It is but reason we should at least not flatter ourselves with fond and too kind opinions.

5. Every day call to mind some one of thy foulest sins, or the most shameful of thy disgraces, or the indiscreetest of thy actions, or anything that did then most trouble thee, and apply it to the present swelling of thy spirit and opinion, and it may help to allay it.

6. Pray often for His grace, by way of confession to God, and reflection upon thyself.

7. Avoid those states, where many ceremonies and circumstances will seem necessary, as will destroy the sobriety of thy thoughts. And certain it is, God is as much glorified by thy example of humility in a low or temperate condition, as by thy bounty in a great and dangerous.

8. Spiritual pride is very dangerous, not only by reason it spoils so many graces, by which we drew nigh unto the kingdom of God, but also because it so frequently creeps upon the spirit of holy persons. For it is no wonder for a beggar to call himself poor, or a drunkard to confess that he is no sober person; but for a holy person to be humble, for one whom all men esteem a saint to fear lest him-

self become a devil, and to observe his own danger, and to discern his own infirmities, and make discovery of his bad adherences, is hard.

9. Often meditate upon the effects of pride on one side, and humility on the other. First, that pride is like a canker, and destroys the beauty of the fairest flowers, the most excellent gifts and graces; but humility crowns them all. Secondly, that pride is a great hindrance to perceiving the things of God,[21] and humility an excellent instrument of spiritual wisdom. Thirdly, that pride hinders the acceptation of our prayers. Fourthly, that humility is but a speaking truth, and all pride is a lie. Fifthly, that humility is the most certain way to real honour, and pride is ever affronted or despised. Sixthly, that pride turned Lucifer into a devil, and humility exalted the Son of God above every name. Seventhly, that 'God resisteth the proud',[22] but 'giveth grace to the humble'; tranquillity of spirit, patience in afflictions, love abroad, peace at home, and utter freedom from contention, and the sin of censuring others, and the trouble of being censured themselves. For the humble man will not judge his brother for the mote in his eye, being more troubled at the beam in his own eye.

10. Remember the blessed Saviour of the world, His whole life being a great continued example of humility. And it were a good design, and yet but reasonable, that we should be as humble, in the midst of our greatest imperfections and basest sins, as Christ was in the midst of His fullness of the Spirit, great wisdom, perfect life, and most admirable virtues.

11. Drive away all flatterers from thy company.

12. Never change thy employment for the sudden coming of another to thee; but if modesty permits, or discretion, appear to him that visits thee the same that thou wert to God and thyself in thy privacy. But if thou wert walking or sleeping, or in any other innocent employment or retirement, snatch not up a book to seem studious, nor fall on thy knees to seem devout, nor alter anything to make him believe thee better employed than thou wert.

13. He who would preserve his humility should choose some spiritual person to whom he shall oblige himself to discover his very thoughts and fancies, every act of his, and all his intercourse with

others in which there may be danger; that by such an openness of spirit he may expose every blast of vainglory, every idle thought, to be chastened and lessened by the rod of spiritual discipline.

14. Who would run into a river, deep and dangerous, with a great burden upon his back, even when he were told of the danger, and earnestly importuned not to do it? Who, knowing the laws of God, the rewards of virtue, the cursed consequences of sin, that it is an evil spirit that tempts him to it, that it is his own destruction that he is then working; that the pleasures of his sin are base and brutish, unsatisfying in the enjoyment, soon over, shameful in their story, bitter in the memory, painful in the effect here, and intolerable for ever; yet in despite of all this, he runs foolishly into his sin and his ruin, merely because he is a fool, and winks hard, and rushes violently like a horse into the battle, or, like a madman, to his death.

If you would try how your soul is grown, you shall know that humility, like the root of a goodly tree, is thrust very far into the ground by these goodly fruits which appear above ground:

Signs of humility
The humble man trusts not to his own discretion, but relies rather upon the judgment of his friends, counsellors, or spiritual guides. He does not pertinaciously pursue the choice of his own will, but in all things lets God choose for him, and his superiors, in those things which concern them. He does not murmur against commands. He is not inquisitive into the reasonableness of indifferent and innocent commands, but believes their command to be reason enough in such cases to exact his obedience. He lives according to a rule, and with compliance to public customs, without any affectation or singularity. He is meek and indifferent in all accidents and chances. He patiently bears injuries. He is always unsatisfied in his own conduct, resolutions, and counsels. He is a great lover of good men, and a praiser of wise men, and a censurer of no man. He is modest in his speech, and reserved in his laughter. He fears, when he hears himself commended, lest God make another judgment concerning his actions than men do. He gives no pert or saucy answers when he is reproved, whether justly or unjustly. He loves to sit down in private and, if he may, he

refuses the temptations of offices and new honours. He is ingenuous, free, and open in his actions and discourses. He mends his fault, and gives thanks when he is admonished. He is ready to do good offices to the murderers of his fame, to his slanderers, backbiters, and detracters, as Christ washed the feet of Judas; and is contented to be suspected of indiscretion, so long as before God he may be really innocent, and not offensive to his neighbour, nor wanting to his just and prudent interest.

V OF MODESTY

Modesty is the appendage of sobriety, and is to chastity, to temperance, and to humility, as the fringes are to a garment. It is a grace of God, that moderates the over-activeness and curiosity of the mind, and orders the passions of the body, and external actions, and is directly opposed to curiosity, to boldness, to undecency. The practice of modesty consists in these following rules.

Acts and duties of modesty, as it is opposed to curiosity
1. Enquire not into the secrets of God[23] but be content to learn thy duty; but if thou beest a teacher, learn it so as may best enable thee to discharge thy office. God's commandments were proclaimed to all the world; but God's counsels are to Himself and to His secret ones, when they are admitted within the veil.

2. Enquire not into the things which are too hard for thee, but learn modestly to know thy infirmities and abilities[24] and raise not thy mind up to inquire into mysteries of state, or the secrets of government, or difficulties theological, if thy employment really be, or thy understanding be judged to be, of a lower rank.

3. Let us not enquire into the affairs of others that concern us not, but be busied within ourselves and our own spheres; ever remembering that to pry into the actions or interests of other men not under our charge, may minister to pride, to tyranny, to uncharitableness, to trouble, but can never consist with modesty; unless where duty or the mere intentions of charity and relation do warrant it.

4. Never listen at the doors or windows;[25] for, besides that it con-

tains in it danger and a snare, it is also an invading my neighbour's privacy.

Every man hath in his own life sins enough, in his own mind trouble enough, in his own fortune evils enough, and in performance of his offices failings more than enough, to entertain his own inquiry. What is it to me if my neighbour's grandfather were a Syrian, or his grandmother illegitimate? Or that another is indebted five thousand pounds, or whether his wife be expensive? But commonly inquisitive persons, or (as the apostle's phrase is) 'busybodies' are not solicitous or inquisitive into the beauty and order of a well-governed family, or after the virtues of an excellent person; but if there be anything for which men keep locks and bars, and porters, things that blush to see the light, and either are shameful in manners, or private in nature, these things are their care and their business. But if great things will satisfy our inquiry, the course of the sun and moon, the spots in their faces, the firmament of heaven, and the supposed orbs, the ebbing and flowing of the sea, are work enough for us. If these be too troublesome, search lower, and tell me why this turf this year brings forth a daisy, and the next year a plaintain; why the apple bears his seed in his heart, and wheat bears it in his head: let him tell why a graft, taking nourishment from a crab-stock, shall have a fruit more noble than its nurse and parent: let him say why the best of oil is at the top, the best of wine in the middle, and best of honey at the bottom, otherwise than it is in some liquors that are thinner, and in some that are thicker. But these things are not such as please busybodies; they must feed upon tragedies, and stories of misfortunes, and crimes: and unless you tell them something sad and new, something that is done within the bounds of their own knowledge or relation, it seems tedious and unsatisfying; which shows plainly it is an evil spirit: envy and idleness married together, and begot curiosity. If a physician should go from house to house unsent for, and inquire what woman hath a cancer, or what man hath a fistula though he could pretend to cure it, he would be almost as unwelcome as the disease itself: and therefore it is inhuman to enquire after crimes and disasters without pretence of amending them, but only to discover them.

Curiosity is the direct incontinency of the spirit; and adultery itself in its principle is many times nothing but a curious inquisition after, and envying of another man's enclosed pleasures; and there have been many who refused fairer objects, that they might ravish an enclosed woman from her retirement and single possessor. For as men clap their garments close about them, when the searching and saucy winds would discover their nakedness; as knowing that what men willingly hear they do willingly speak of. Knock, therefore, at the door before you enter upon your neighbour's privacy; and remember that there is no difference between entering into his house, and looking into it.

Acts of modesty, as it is opposed to boldness

1. Let us always bear about us such reverence and fear of God as to tremble at His voice, to express our apprehensions of His greatness.

2. Be reverent, modest, and reserved, giving to all according to their quality, keeping distance, speaking little, answering pertinently, not interposing without leave or reason; and ever present the fairest side of thy discourse, of thy temper, of thy ceremony, as being ashamed to serve excellent persons with unhandsome intercourse.

3. Never lie before a king or a great person, nor stand in a lie, when thou art accused; nor offer to justify what is indeed a fault; but modestly be ashamed of it, ask pardon, and make amends.

4. Never boast of thy sin, but at least lay a veil upon thy nakedness and shame. Have this beginning of repentance, to believe thy sin to be shame. For he that blushes not at his crime, but adds shamelessness to his shame, hath no instrument left to restore him to the hopes of virtue.

5. Be not confident and affirmative in an uncertain matter, but report things modestly and temperately, according to the authority, or the reason inducing thee.

6. Pretend not to more knowledge than thou hast,[26] but be content to seem ignorant where thou art so, lest thou beest either brought to shame, or retirest into shamelessness.

Acts of modesty, as it is opposed to indecency

1. In your prayers, in churches and places of religion, use reverent

postures, great attention, grave ceremony, remembering that we speak to God, in our reverence to whom we cannot possibly exceed; that is, let it be the best.

2. Use those forms of salutation, reverence, and decency, which custom prescribes, and is usual amongst the most sober persons; giving honour to whom honour belongeth.

3. Be not merry at a funeral, nor sad upon a festival; but rejoice with them that rejoice, and weep with them that weep.

4. Abstain from wanton and dissolute laughter, petulant and uncomely jests, loud talking, jeering, and all such actions, which in civil account are called undecencies and incivilities.

5. Towards your parents use all modesty of duty and humble carriage; towards them and all your kindred, be severe in the modesties of chastity; ever fearing, lest the freedoms of natural kindness should enlarge into any neighbourhood of unhandsome-ness.

6. Be a curious observer of all those things which are of good report, and are parts of public honesty.[27] For charity requires us to comply with those fancies and affections which are agreeable to nature, or the analogy of virtue, or public laws, or old customs. It is against modesty for a woman to marry a second husband as long as she bears a burden by the first, or to admit a second love while her funeral tears are not wiped from her cheeks. It is against public honesty to do some lawful actions of privacy in public, and therefore in such cases retirement is a duty of modesty.

7. Be grave, decent, and modest, in thy clothing and ornament: never let it be above thy condition, not always equal to it, never light or amorous, never discovering a nakedness through a thin veil, which thou pretendest to hide; never to lay a snare for a soul; but remember what becomes a Christian, professing holiness, chastity, and the discipline of the holy Jesus: and the first effects of this let your servants feel, by your gentleness and aptness to be pleased with their usual diligence and ordinary conduct.

8. Hither also is to be reduced singular and affected walking; proud, nice, and ridiculous gestures of body, paintings and lascivious dressings. And this duty of modesty, is expressly enjoined to all

Christian women by St. Paul: 'That women adorn themselves in
modest apparel'.[28]

9. As those meats are to be avoided which tempt our stomachs
beyond our hunger, so also should prudent persons decline all those
spectacles, relations, theatres, loud noises and outcries, which concern
us not, and are beside our natural or moral interest. Our senses
should not, like petulant and wanton girls, wander into markets and
theatres without just employment; but when they are sent abroad by
reason, return quickly with their errand, and remain modestly at
home under their guide till they be sent again.

10. Let all persons observe modesty towards themselves, in the
handsome treatment of their own body, and such as are in their
power, whether living or dead. Against this rule they offend who
expose to others their own, or pry into others' nakedness beyond the
limits of necessity, or where a leave is not made holy by a permission
from God. In all these cases and particulars, although they seem little,
yet our duty and concernment is not little: 'He that despiseth little
things shall perish by little and little'.[29]

VI CONTENTEDNESS IN ALL ESTATES AND ACCIDENTS

Virtues and discourses are, like friends, necessary in all fortunes; but
those are the best, which are friends in our sadnesses, and support us
in our sorrows and sad accidents: and in this sense, no man that is
virtuous can be friendless; nor hath any man reason to complain of
the divine providence, or accuse the public disorder of things, or his
own infelicity, since God hath appointed one remedy for all the
evils in the world, and that is a contented spirit: for this alone makes
a man pass through fire, and not be scorched; through seas, and not
be drowned; through hunger and nakedness, and want nothing. For
since all the evil in the world consists in the disagreeing between the
object and the appetite, as when a man hath what he desires not, or
desires what he hath not, or desires amiss; he that composes his spirit
to the present accident, hath variety of instances for his virtue, but
none to trouble him, because his desires enlarge not beyond his

present fortune. For there is some virtue or other to be exercised, whatever happens, either patience or thanksgiving, love or fear, moderation or humility, charity or contentedness, and they are every one of them equally in order to immortal felicity. Beauty is not made by white or red, by black eyes and a round face, by a straight body and a smooth skin; but by a proportion to the fancy. No rules can make amiability, our minds and apprehensions make that; and so is our felicity; and we may be reconciled to poverty and a low fortune, if we suffer contentedness and the grace of God to make the proportions. For no man is poor that does not think himself so: but if in a full fortune with impatience he desires more, he proclaims his wants and his beggarly condition. But because this grace of contentedness was the sum of all the old moral philosophy, and a great duty in Christianity, and of most universal use in the whole course of our lives, and the only instrument to ease the burdens of the world and the enmities of sad chances, it will not be amiss to press it by the proper arguments by which God hath bound it upon our spirits; it being fastened by reason and religion, by duty and interest, by necessity and conveniency, by example, and by the proposition of excellent rewards, no less than peace and felicity.

1. Contentedness in all estates is a duty of religion; it is the great reasonableness of complying with the divine providence which governs all the world, and hath so ordered us in the administration of His great family. He were a strange fool that should be angry because dogs and sheep need no shoes, and yet himself is full of care to get some. God hath supplied those needs to them by natural provisions, and to thee by an artificial: for He hath given thee reason to learn a trade, or some means to make or buy them, so that it only differs in the manner of our provision: and which had you rather want, shoes or reason? And my patron, that hath given me a farm, is freer to me than if he gives a loaf ready baked. But, however, all these gifts come from Him, and if we murmur here we may at the next melancholy be troubled that God did not make us to be angels or stars. For if that which we are or have, do not content us, we may be troubled for everything in the world which is besides our being or our possessions.

God is the master of the scenes; we must not choose which part we shall act; it concerns us only to be careful that we do it well, always saying, 'If this please God, let it be as it is': we, who pray that God's will may be done in earth as it is in heaven.

For is not all the world God's family? Are not we His creatures? Do we not live upon His meat, and move by His strength, and do our work by His light? And shall there be a mutiny among the flocks and herds, because their lord or their shepherd chooses their pastures, and suffers them not to wander into deserts and unknown ways? If we choose, we do it so foolishly that we cannot like it long, and most commonly not at all; but God is wise, affectionate to our needs, and powerful. Here, therefore, is the wisdom of the contented man, to let God choose for him; for when we have given up our wills to Him, our spirits must needs rest, while our conditions have for their security the power, the wisdom, and the charity of God.

2. Contentedness in all accidents brings great peace of spirit, and is the great and only instrument of temporal felicity. It removes the sting from the accident, and makes a man not to depend upon chance and the uncertain dispositions of men for his well-being, but only on God and His own spirit. We ourselves make our fortunes good or bad. If we fear to die, or know not to be patient, or are proud or covetous, then calamity sits heavy on us. But if we know how to manage a noble principle, and fear not death so much as a dishonest action, and think impatience a worse evil than a fever, and pride to be the biggest disgrace, and poverty to be infinitely desirable before the torments of covetousness, then we shall quickly be of another mind.

But no man can be happy that hath great hopes and great fears of things without, and events depending upon other men, or upon the chances of fortune. He that suffers a transporting passion concerning things within the power of others, is free from sorrow and amazement no longer than his enemy shall give him leave; and it is ten to one but he shall be smitten then and there, where it shall most trouble. The old Stoics, when you told them of a sad story, would still answer, 'What is that to me? Yes, for the tyrant hath sentenced you also to prison. Well, what is that? he will put a chain upon my leg; but he cannot bind my soul': This, in Gentile philosophy, is the same with the discourse of St. Paul, 'I have learned, in whatsoever state I am, therewith to be content. I know both how to be abased, and I know how to abound: everywhere and in all things I am instructed, both to be full and to be hungry; both to abound and to suffer need'.[30]

We are in the world like men playing at tables; the chance is not in our power, but to play it is; and when it is fallen we must manage it as we can; and let nothing trouble us but when we do a base action, or speak like a fool, or think wickedly: these things God hath put into our powers; but concerning those things which are wholly in the choice of another, they cannot fall under our deliberation, and therefore neither are they fit for our passions. Therefore, if thou hast lost thy land, do not also lose thy constancy; and if thou must die a little sooner, yet do not die impatiently. For no chance is evil to him that is content; and to a man nothing is miserable unless it be unreasonable. No man can make another man to be his slave unless he hath first enslaved himself to life and death, to pleasure or pain, to hope or fear: command these passions, and you are freer than the Parthian kings.

Exercises to procure contentedness

Upon the strength of these premises, we may reduce this virtue to practice.

1. When anything happens to our displeasure, let us endeavour to take off its trouble by turning it into spiritual or artificial advantage. 'The ox, when he is weary, treads surest'; and if there be nothing else in the disgrace, but that it makes us to walk warily, and tread sure for fear of our enemies, that is better than to be flattered into pride and carelessness.

If, therefore, thou fallest from thy employment in public, take sanctuary in an honest retirement, being indifferent to thy gain abroad, or thy safety at home. If thou art out of favour with thy prince, secure the favour of the King of kings, and then there is no harm come to thee. When the north wind blows hard, and it rains sadly, none but fools sit down in it and cry; wise people defend themselves against it with a warm garment, or a good fire and a dry roof. When a storm of a sad mischance beats upon our spirits, turn it into some advantage by observing where it can serve another end, either of religion or prudence, of more safety or less envy: at least it may make us weary of the world's vanity, and make our spirits to dwell in those regions where content dwells essentially. If it does any good to our souls, it hath made more than sufficient recompense for all the temporal affliction. We have put our conditions past the power of chance; and this was called, in the old Greek comedy, 'a being revenged on fortune by becoming philosophers', and turning the chance into reason or religion: for so a wise man shall overrule his stars, and have a greater influence upon his own content than all the constellations and planets of the firmament.

2. Never compare thy condition with those above thee; but, to secure thy content, look upon those thousands with whom thou wouldest not for any interest change thy fortune and condition. There are but a few kings among mankind, but many thousands who are very miserable if compared to thee. However, it is a huge folly rather to grieve for the good of others than to rejoice for that good which God hath given us of our own.

And yet there is no wise or good man that would change persons or conditions entirely with any man in the world. It may be he would have one man's wealth added to himself, or the power of a second, or the learning of a third; but still he would receive these into his own person, because he loves that best, and therefore esteems it best, and therefore over-values all that which he is, before all that which any other man in the world can be. For every man hath desires of his own, and objects just fitted to them, without which he cannot be, unless he were not himself. Either change all or none. Cease to love yourself best, or be content with that portion of being and blessing for which you love yourself so well.

3. It conduces much to our content, if we pass by those things which happen to our trouble, and consider that which is pleasing and prosperous, that by the representation of the better, the worse may be blotted out. Or else please thyself with hopes of the future; for we were not born with this sadness upon us, and it was a change that brought us into it, and a change may bring us out again. Harvest will come, and then every farmer is rich, at least for a month or two.

It may be thou art entered into the cloud which will bring a gentle shower to refresh thy sorrows.

Now suppose thyself in as great a sadness as ever did load thy spirit, wouldst thou not bear it cheerfully and nobly if thou wert sure that within a certain space some strange excellent fortune would relieve thee, and enrich thee so as to overflow all thy hopes and thy desires and capacities? Now, then, when a sadness lies heavy upon thee, remember that thou art a Christian designed to the inheritance of Jesus. Indeed if thou thinkest thou shalt perish, I cannot blame thee to be sad, sad till thy heartstrings crack. But if thou believest thou shalt be saved, consider how great is that joy, how unspeakable is the glory, how excellent is the recompense for all the sufferings in the world, if they were all laden upon the spirit? So that, let thy condition be what it will, here thou art but a stranger, travelling to thy country, where the glories of a kingdom are prepared for thee; it is therefore a huge folly to be much afflicted because thou hast a less convenient inn to lodge in by the way.

But these arts of looking forwards and backwards are more than enough to support the spirit of a Christian: there is no man but hath blessings enough in present possession to outweigh the evils of a great affliction. If you miss an office for which you stood candidate, then, besides that you are quit of the cares and the envy of it, you still have all those excellences which rendered you capable to receive it, and they are better than the best office in the commonwealth. If your estate be lessened, you need the less to care who governs the province, whether he be rude or gentle. If I fall into the hands of thieves, or of publicans and sequestrators: what now? They have left me the sun and moon, fire and water, a loving wife, and many friends to pity me, and some to relieve me, and I can still discourse; and unless I list, they have not taken away my merry countenance, and my cheerful spirit, and a good conscience: they still have left me the providence of God, and all the promises of the gospel, and my religion, and my hopes of heaven, and my charity to them too; and still I sleep and digest, I eat and drink, I read and meditate; I can walk in my neighbour's pleasant fields, and see the varieties of natural beauties, and delight in all that in which God delights—that is, in virtue and wisdom, in the whole creation, and in God Himself. And he that hath so many causes of joy, and so great, is very much in love with sorrow and peevishness, who loses all these pleasures, and chooses to sit down upon his little handful of thorns. He deserves to starve in the midst of plenty, and to want comfort while he is encircled with blessings.

4. Enjoy the present, whatsoever it be, and be not solicitous for the future; for if you take your foot from the present standing, and thrust it forward towards to-morrow's event, you are in a restless condition: it is like refusing to quench your present thirst by fearing you shall want drink the next day. If it be well today, it is madness to make the present miserable by fearing it may be ill tomorrow. Let your trouble tarry till its own day comes. Enjoy the blessings of this day, if God sends them, and the evils of it bear patiently and sweetly; for this day is only ours; we are dead to yesterday, and we are not yet born to the morrow. He therefore that enjoys the present if it be good, enjoys as much as is possible. 'Sufficient to the day' (said Christ) 'is the evil thereof': sufficient, but not intolerable. Miserable is he who thrusts his passions forwards, towards future events, and suffers all that he may enjoy to be lost, thinking nothing fit to be enjoyed but that which is not or cannot be had.

5. Let us prepare our minds against changes, always expecting them, that we be not surprised when they come; for nothing is so great an enemy to tranquillity and a contented spirit as unreadiness when our fortunes are violently changed. Our spirits are unchanged if they always stood in the suburbs and expectation of sorrows. The apostles, who every day knocked at the gate of death, and looked upon it continually, went to their martyrdom in peace and evenness.

6. Consider how desirable health is to a sick man, or liberty to a prisoner; and if but a fit of the toothache seize us with violence, all those troubles, which in our health afflicted us, disband instantly, and seem inconsiderable. Remember then that God had given thee a blessing the want of which is infinitely more trouble than thy present debt, or poverty, or loss. The very privative blessings, the blessings of immunity, safeguard, liberty, and integrity, which we commonly enjoy, deserve the thanksgiving of a whole life. I have known an affectionate wife, when she hath been in fear of parting with

her beloved husband, heartily desire of God his life or society upon any conditions that were not sinful; and choose to beg with him rather than to feast without him. What wise man in the world is there who does not prefer a small fortune with peace before a great one with contention, and war, and violence? And then he is no longer wise if he alters his opinion when he hath his wish.

7. If you will secure a contented spirit, you must measure your desires by your fortune and condition, not your fortunes by your desires: that is, be governed by your needs, not by your fancy; by nature, not by evil customs and ambitious principles. Can a man quench his thirst better out of a river or a full urn, or drink better from the fountain, which is finely paved with marble, than when it swells over the green turf? Pride and artificial gluttonies do but adulterate nature, making our diet healthless, our appetites impatient and unsatisfiable, and the taste mixed, fantastical, and meretricious. But when we create needs that God or nature never made, we have erected to ourselves an infinite stock of trouble that can have no end. God and nature made no more needs than they mean to satisfy; and he that will make more must look for satisfaction where he can.

8. In all troubles and sadder accidents, let us take sanctuary in religion, and by innocence cast out anchors for our souls, to keep them from shipwreck, though they be not kept from storm. St. Paul's character is engraved in the forehead of our fortune; 'We are troubled on every side, but not distressed; perplexed, but not in despair; persecuted, but not forsaken; cast down, but not destroyed'.[31] 'And who is he that will harm you, if ye be followers of that which is good'?[32] For indeed everything in the world is indifferent, but sin. The greatest evils are from within us; and from ourselves also we must look for our greatest good; for God is the fountain of it, but reaches it to us by our own hands; and when all things look sadly round about us, then only we shall find, how excellent a fortune it is to have God to our friend; and, of all friendships, that only is created to support us in our needs. For it is sin that turns fear into despair, anger into rage, and loss into madness, and sorrow to amazement and confusion.

Let us not therefore be governed by external, and present, and seeming things; nor make other men, and they not the wisest, to be judges of our felicity, so that we be happy or miserable as they please to think us : but let reason, and experience, and religion, and hope relying upon the Divine promises, be the measure of our judgment. No wise man did ever describe felicity without virtue ; and no good man did ever think virtue could depend upon the variety of a good or bad fortune. It is no evil to be poor, but to be vicious and impatient.

Means to obtain content

To these exercises and spiritual instruments if we add the following considerations concerning the nature and circumstances of human chance, we may better secure our peace. For as to children, who are afraid of vain images, we use to persuade confidence by making them to handle and look nearer such things, that when in such a familiarity, they perceive them innocent, they may overcome their fears.

1. Consider that the universal providence of God hath so ordered it, that the good things of nature and fortune are divided, that we may know how to bear our own and relieve each other's wants and imperfections. He supports my poverty with his wealth; I counsel and instruct him with my learning and experience. He hath many friends, I many children; he hath no heir, I have no inheritance; and any one great blessing, together with the common portions of nature and necessity, is a fair fortune, if it be but health or strength, or the swiftness of Ahimaaz. For it is an unreasonable discontent to be troubled that I have not so good cocks or dogs or horses as my neighbour, being more troubled that I want one thing that I need not, than thankful for having received all that I need.

There are some instances of fortune and a fair condition that cannot stand with some others. If you covet learning, you must have leisure and a retired life ; if to be a politician, you must go abroad and get experience, and do all businesses, and keep all company, and have no leisure at all. If you will be rich, you must be frugal ; if you will be popular, you must be bountiful ; if a philosopher, you must despise riches. The Greek that designed to make the most exquisite picture that could be imagined, fancied the eye of Chione, and the hair of Paegnium, and Tarsia's lip, Philenium's chin, and the forehead of

Delphia, and set all these upon Milphidippa's neck, and thought that
he should outdo both art and nature. But when he came to view the
proportions, he found that although, singly, they were rare pieces, yet
in the whole they made a most ugly face. The dispersed excellences
and blessings of many men, if given to one, would not make a handsome but a monstrous fortune. Use therefore that faculty which nature
hath given thee, and thy education hath made actual, and thy calling
hath made a duty. But if thou desirest to be a saint, refuse not his
persecution.

2. Consider how many excellent personages in all ages have
suffered as great or greater calamities than this which now tempts thee
to impatience. Almost all the ages of the world have noted that their
most eminent scholars were most eminently poor, some by choice,
but most by chance. In women, the sharpest pains of childbirth, show
that there is no state exempt from sorrow. The weakest persons have
strength more than enough to bear the greatest evil; and the greatest
queens, and the mothers of saints and apostles, have no charter of
exemption. But the Lord of men and angels was also the King of
sufferings; and if thy coarse robe trouble thee, remember the swadd-
ling-clothes of Jesus; if thy bed be uneasy, yet it is not worse than
His manger; and He suffered all the sorrows which we deserved. We
therefore have great reason to sit down upon our own hearths, and
warm ourselves at our own fires, and feed upon content at home.

In the most beauteous and splendid fortune there are many cares.
In the fortune of a prince there is not the coarse robe of beggary, but
there are infinite cares; and the judge sits upon the tribunal with great
ceremony and ostentation of fortune, and yet, at his house or in his
breast there is something that causes him to sigh deeply. Pittacus was
a wise and valiant man, but his wife overthrew the table when he had
invited his friends; upon which the good man, to excuse her incivility, and his own misfortune, said 'that every man had one evil,
and he was most happy that had but that alone'. And if nothing else
happens, yet sicknesses so often do embitter the fortune and content
of a family, that a physician in a few years, and with the practice upon
a very few families, gets experience enough to administer to almost
all diseases. And when thy little misfortune troubles thee, remember

that thou hast known the best of kings and the best of men put to death publicly by his own subjects.

3. It may be I am slighted, or I have received ill language; but my head aches not for it, neither hath it broke my thigh, nor taken away my virtue, unless I lose my charity or my patience. Inquire, therefore, what you are the worse, either in soul or in body, for what hath happened; for upon this very stock many evils will disappear, since the body and the soul make up the whole man.

4. Consider that sad accidents and a state of affliction is a school of virtue; 'It is good for me (said David) that I have been afflicted, for thereby I have learned Thy law'.[33] For God, who in mercy and wisdom governs, the world, would never have suffered so many sadnesses, and have sent them especially to the most virtuous and the wisest men, but that they should be the nursery of virtue, the exercise of wisdom, the trial of patience, the venturing for a crown, and the gate of glory.

5. Consider that afflictions are oftentimes the occasions of great temporal advantages; and we must not look upon them as they sit down heavily upon us, but as they serve some of God's ends, and the purposes of universal Providence. He brings good out of evil; and therefore it were but reason we should trust God to govern His own world as He pleases; and that we should patiently wait till the change cometh, or the reason be discovered.

6. For it is but reasonable to bear accident patiently since impatience does but entangle us, like the fluttering of a bird in a net, but cannot at all ease our trouble, or prevent the accident: it must be run through, and therefore it were better we compose ourselves to a patient than to a troubled and miserable suffering.

7. However, if you will not otherwise be cured, time at last will do it alone; and then consider, do you mean to mourn always, or but for a time? If always, you are miserable and foolish. If for a time, then why will you not apply those reasons to your grief at first with which you will cure it at last? And here let the worst thing happen that can, it will end in death, and we commonly think that to be near enough.

8. Lastly, of those things which are reckoned amongst evils, some are better than their contraries; and to a good man the very worst is tolerable.

Poverty or a low fortune

1. Poverty is better than riches, and a mean fortune to be chosen before a great and splendid one. It is indeed despised, and makes men contemptible; it exposes a man to the insolence of evil persons, and leaves a man defenceless; it is always suspected; its stories are accounted lies, and all its counsels follies: it puts a man from all employment: it makes a man's discourses tedious, and his society troublesome. This is the worst of it: and yet all this, and far worse the apostles suffered for being Christians; and Christianity itself may be esteemed an affliction as well as poverty, if this be all that can be said against it; for the apostles and the most eminent Christians were really poor, and were used contemptuously: and yet, that poverty is despised may be an argument to commend it, if it be despised by none but persons vicious and ignorant. A great fortune is a great vanity, and riches nothing but danger, trouble, and temptation. But poverty is the sister of a good mind, the parent of sober counsels, and the nurse of all virtue.

For what is it that you admire in the fortune of a great king? Is it that he always goes in a great company? You may thirst yourself into the same crowd, or go often to church, and have as great company as he. Pomp, and the other circumstances of his distance, are not made for him, but for his subjects, that they may separate him from common usages, and be taught to be governed. If you look upon fine things in themselves you shall consider that they cannot cure the toothache, nor make one wise, nor fill the belly, nor give one night's sleep (though they help to break many) —not satisfying any appetite of nature, or reason, or religion; but they are states of greatness which only make it possible for a man to be made extremely miserable. A great estate hath great crosses, and a mean fortune hath but small ones.

Now in the state of poverty, there is nothing to be accounted for but the fear of wanting necessaries; of which if a man could be secured, he might live free from care. But there must needs be great security to all Christians, since Christ not only made express promises that we should have sufficient for this life, but also took great pains and used many arguments to create confidence in us; and such they were, which by their own strength were sufficient, though you abate the authority of the speaker. 'Take no thought, for your life, what ye shall eat, or what ye shall drink, nor yet for your body, what ye shall put on. Is not the life more than meat, and the body than raiment? Behold the fowls of the air, for they sow not, neither do they reap, nor gather into barns, yet your heavenly Father feedeth them. Are ye not not much better than they? Which of you, by taking thought, can add one cubit to his stature? And why take ye thought for raiment? Consider the lilies of the field, how they grow—they toil not, neither do they spin; and yet I say unto you, that even Solomon in all his glory was not arrayed like one of these. Therefore, if God so clothe the grass of the field, which today is and tomorrow is cast into the oven, shall he not much more clothe you, O ye of little faith? Therefore take no thought, saying, What shall we eat, or what shall we drink, or wherewithal shall we be clothed? (for after all these things do the Gentiles seek); for your heavenly Father knoweth that ye have need of all these things. But seek ye first the kingdom of God and His righteousness, and all these things shall be added unto you. Take therefore no thought for the morrow, for the morrow shall take thought for the things of itself: sufficient to the day is the evil thereof'.[34] So St. Paul: 'Be careful for nothing; but in everything by prayer and supplication, with thanksgiving, let your requests be made known unto God'.[35] And again, 'Charge them that are rich in this world that they be not highminded, nor trust in uncertain riches, but in the living God, who giveth us richly all things, to enjoy'.[36] And yet again, 'Let your conversation be without covetousness, and be content with such things as ye have'.[37] And all this is by St. Peter summed up in our duty thus: 'Casting all your care upon Him, for He careth for you'. Which words he seems to have borrowed out of the fifty-fifth Psalm, ver. 23, where David saith the same thing almost in the same words. To which I only add the observation made by him, and the argument of experience: 'I have been young, and now am old, and yet saw I never the righteous forsaken, nor his seed begging their bread'.

And now, after all this, a fearless confidence in God, concerning a provision of necessaries, is so reasonable that it becomes a duty; and he is scarce a Christian whose faith is so little as to be suspicious con-

cerning meat and clothes: that man hath nothing in him of the nobleness or confidence of charity. But besides the reasonableness of this
faith and this hope, we have infinite experience of it. How innocent,
how careless, how secure is infancy! and yet how certainly provided
for! We have lived at God's charges all the days of our life, and
hitherto He hath not failed us. Add to this, that God hath given us His
Holy Spirit; He hath promised heaven to us; He hath given us His
Son; and we are taught from Scripture to make this inference from
hence, 'How should not He with Him freely give us all things'?

The charge of many children

We have a title to be provided for as we are God's creatures, and as
we are His children. Therefore it is a huge folly and infidelity to be
troubled and full of care because we have many children. Every child
is a new title to God's care and providence; so that many children are
a great wealth. Titius keeps ten ploughs, Cornelia hath ten children.
His hinds and horses eat up all his corn, and her children are sufficiently maintained with her little. They bring in and eat up, and she
indeed eats up, but they also bring in from the storehouses of heaven,
and the granaries of God; and my children are not so much mine as
they are God's: He feeds them in the womb by ways secret and in-
sensible; and would not work a perpetual miracle to bring them
forth, and then to starve them.

Violent necessities

But some men are highly tempted, and are brought to a strait, that
without a miracle they cannot be relieved; what shall they do? If it
be innocent, God does usually relieve such necessities; and He does
not only upon our prayers grant us more than He promised of temporal things, but also He gives many times more than we ask. This
is no object for our faith, but ground enough for a temporal and
prudent hope. Only we must remember that our portion of temporal
things is but food and raiment. God hath not promised us coaches
and horses, rich houses and jewels, Tyrian silks and Persian carpets;
neither hath He promised to minister to our needs in such circum-

stances as we shall appoint, but such as Himself shall choose. But if He takes away the flesh-pots from thee, He can also alter the appetite, and He hath given thee power and commandment to restrain it. For the grace of God secures you of provisions, and yet the grace of God feeds and supports the spirit in the want of provisions. Poverty therefore is in some senses eligible, and to be preferred before riches; but in all senses it is very tolerable.

Death of children, or nearest relatives and friends

There are some persons who have been noted for excellent in their lives and passions, rarely innocent, and yet hugely penitent for indiscretions and harmless infirmities; such as was Paulina, one of the ghostly children of St. Jerome; and yet, when any of her children died, she was arrested with a sorrow so great as brought her to the edge of her grave. And the more tender our spirits are made by religion, the more easy we are to let in grief. To cure which, we may consider that all the world must die, and therefore to be impatient at the death of a person is to mourn because thy friend or child was not born an angel. It is no more than a man does every day: for every night death hath gotten possession of that day, and we shall never live that day over again; and when the last day is come, there are no more days left for us to die. And what is sleeping and waking, but living and dying? what is spring and autumn, youth and old age, morning and evening, but real images of life and death?

Untimely death

It is not mere dying that is the cause of impatient mourning; but that the child died young, before he knew good and evil, his right hand from his left, and so lost all his portion of this world, and they know not of what excellency his portion in the next shall be. If he died young, he lost but little, for he understood but little, and had not capacities of great pleasures or great cares; but yet he died innocent, and before the sweetness of his soul was defloured and ravished from him by the flames and follies of a froward age. You had a son born; and if you reckon that for evil, you are unthankful for the blessing; if it be good, it is better that you had the blessing for a while, than not at all; and yet, if he had never been born, this sorrow had not been at all. But be no more displeased at God for giving you a blessing for a while than you would have been if He had not given it at all; and if it be a good, turn it not into sorrow and sadness. But if we have great reason to complain of the calamities and evils, of our life, then we have the less reason to grieve that those whom we loved have so small a portion of evil assigned to them. A blessed immortality is rendered to them secure, if our children die young, being snatched from the dangers of an evil choice, and carried to their little cells of felicity, where they can weep no more. And possibly we may doubt concerning Christian men and women, but we cannot suspect that to Christian infants death can be such an evil, but that it brings to them much more good than it takes from them in this life.

Death unseasonable

Others can well bear the death of infants, but when they have spent some years of childhood or youth, and are entered into arts and society, when they are hopeful and provided for, when the parents are to reap the comfort of all their fears and cares, then it breaks the spirit to lose them. They miss what they had flattered themselves into by hope and opinion. Since we hope he is gone to God and to rest, it is an ill expression of our love to them that we weep; for that life is not best which is longest, and it shall not be enquired how long they have lived, but how well. And why are we troubled that he had arts and sciences before he died? or are we troubled that he does not live to make use of them? The first is cause of joy, for they are excellent in order to certain ends; and the second cannot be cause of sorrow, because he hath no need to use them, being provided with the manner of eternity. From the time in which a man is conceived, forward to eternity he shall never cease to be: and let him die young or old, still he hath an immortal soul, and hath laid down his body only for a time, as that which was the instrument of his trouble and sorrow, and the scene of sicknesses and disease. The child may with more reason be allowed to cry for leaving his mother's womb for this world, than a man can for changing this world for another.

s are yet troubled at the manner of their child's or friend's death; he was drowned, or lost his head, or died of the plague; and this is a new spring of sorrow. But no man can give a sensible account how it shall be worse for a child to die with drowning in half an hour, than to endure a fever of one-and-twenty days. And if my friend lost his head, so he did not lose his constancy and his religion, he died with huge advantage.

Being childless

But by this means I am left without an heir. Well, suppose that: thou hast no heir, and I have no inheritance; and there are many kings and emperors that have died childless, and Augustus Caesar was forced to adopt his wife's son to inherit all the Roman greatness. And there are many wise persons that never married; and all that inherit anything of Christ's kingdom come to it by adoption, not by natural inheritance.

Evil or unfortunate children

And by this means we are freed from the greater sorrows of having a fool, a swine, or a goat, to rule after us in our families. And yet even this condition admits of comfort. The son of Solomon was but a silly weak man; and the son of Hezekiah was wicked; and all the fools and barbarous people, all the thieves and pirates, all the slaves and miserable men and women of the world, are the sons and daughters of Noah; and we must not look to be exempted from that sorrow; it is enough for us that we bear it evenly.

Our own death

And how if you were to die yourself? You know you must; only be ready for it by the preparations of a good life, and then it is the greatest good that ever happened to thee. Else there is nothing that can comfort you: but if you have served God in a holy life, send away the weepers; tell them it is as much intemperance to weep too much as to laugh too much: and when thou art alone, or with fitting company, die as thou shouldest, but do not die impatiently, and like a fox caught in a trap. For if you fear death, you shall never the more avoid it, but you make it miserable. To die is necessary and natural, and it may be honourable: but to die poorly, and basely, and sinfully, that alone is it that can make a man unfortunate.

Prayers for Christian sobriety

A Prayer against sensuality
O eternal Father, fill my soul with so deep a sense of the excellences of spiritual and heavenly things, that I may, with the prudence of a holy discipline, clear resolutions and a free spirit, have my conversation in heavenly employments; that being, a pilgrim and a stranger here, I may covet after and labour for an abiding city, through Jesus Christ our Lord. Amen.

For temperance
O Almighty God who fillest all things with plenty, teach me to use Thy creatures soberly and temperately, that I may not, with loads of meat or drink, make my spirit unapt for the performance of my duty, or my body healthless, or my affections sensual and unholy. In the strength of Thy provisions may I cheerfully and actively and diligently serve Thee; that I may worthily feast at Thy table here, and through Thy grace, be admitted to Thy table hereafter. Amen.

For chastity; to be said especially by unmarried persons
Almighty God, let Thy gracious and Holy Spirit reprove the spirit of fornication and uncleanness, and cast him out; that my body may be holy. Seal up my senses from all vain objects, and let them be entirely possessed with religion, and fortified with prudence, watchfulness, and mortification; that I, possessing my vessel in holiness, may lay it down with a holy hope, and receive it again in a joyful resurrection, through Jesus Christ our Lord. Amen.

A Prayer for the Love of God, to be said by virgins and widows, professed or resolved so to live: and may be used by any one
O holy and purest Jesus, fill my soul with religion, that I may love Thee as much as ever any creature loved Thee, even with all my soul and all my faculties, and all the degrees of every faculty; let me know no loves but those of duty and charity, obedience and devotion. Give me purity and humility, modesty and devotion, charity and patience, O holy and sweetest Saviour.   Amen.

A Prayer to be said by married persons

O eternal and gracious Father, who hast consecrated the holy estate of marriage to represent the union of Christ and His church, let Thy Holy Spirit so guide me in the doing the duties of this state, that it may not become a sin unto me; nor that liberty become an occasion of licentiousness by my own weakness and sensuality. Let me in all accidents and circumstances, be severe in my duty towards Thee, affectionate and dear to my wife (or husband), a guide and good example to my family, and in all quietness, sobriety, prudence, and peace. And the blessings of the eternal God, be upon the body and soul of Thy servant my wife (or husband), and abide upon her (or him) till the end of a holy and happy life. Amen.

A Prayer for the grace of humility

O holy and most gracious Jesus, who by the practice of a whole life didst command us to be meek and humble, be pleased to give me the grace, as Thou hast given me the commandment. Mortify in me all proud thoughts and vain opinions of myself; let me return to Thee the acknowledgment of all those good things Thou hast given me. Let me go before my brethren in nothing but in striving to do them honour and Thee glory, for Jesus' sake. Amen.

A Prayer for a contented spirit

O Almighty God, Father and Lord of all the creatures, by secret and undiscernible ways bringing good out of evil; give me wisdom from above; teach me to be content in all changes of person and condition, to be temperate in prosperity, and in adversity to be meek, patient, and resigned; and to look through the cloud, in the meantime doing my duty with an unwearied diligence, and an undisturbed resolution, laying up my hopes in heaven and the rewards of holy living, and being strengthened with the spirit of the inner man, through Jesus Christ our Lord. Amen.

NOTES: CHAPTER 2

1   I Cor. IX[25]
2   Ecclus. XXXI[12, 13, 19]
3   Ecclus. XXXI[20]
4   Luke XXI[34]
5   Ecclus. XXXI[25]
6   Prov. XXIII[29, 30] Ecclus. XXXI[26]
7   Prov. XXIII[33]
8   Ephes. V[18]
9   Prov. XXXI[4, 5]
10 I Thess. V[8]
11 I Thess. IV[3-5]
12 Job XXIV[15]
13 Hos. II[6]
14 I Cor. VI[18]
15 Psalm LI
16 I Cor. VI[19]
17 I Cor. III[17] I Cor. VI[10]
18 Ephes. V[32]
19 I Peter I[22]
20 I Cor. VII[5]
21 Matt. XI[25]
22 James IV[6]
23 Ecclus. III[21-23]
24 Prov. XXV
25 Eccles. VII[21]
26 Ecclus. III[25]
27 Phil. IV[8]
28 I Tim. II[9]
29 Ecclus. XIX[1]
30 Phil. IV[11, 12] I Tim. VI[6] Heb. XIII[5]
31 2 Cor. IV[8, 9]
32 I Peter III[13] IV[15, 16]
33 Psalm CXIX[75]
34 Matt. VI[25-34]
35 Phil. IV[6]
36 I Tim. VI[17]
37 Heb. XIII[5, 6]

3 · Christian justice

Justice is by the Christian religion enjoined by two propositions in Scripture: 'Whatsoever ye would that men should do to you, even so do to them'. This is the measure of commutative justice, which supposes exchange of things profitable for things profitable, that as I supply your need you may supply mine; as I do a benefit to you, I may receive one by you. And because every man may be injured by another, therefore his security shall depend upon mine: if he will not let me be safe, he shall not be safe himself (only the manner of his being punished is, upon great reason, both by God and all the world, taken from particulars, and committed to a public disinterested person, who will do justice without passion both to him and to me); if he refuses to do me advantage, he shall receive none when his needs require it. And thus God gave necessities to man, and several abilities to several persons, that they may be knit together by justice, as the parts of the world are by nature. And He hath given us all a sufficient stock of self-love and desire of self-preservation, to be as the chain to tie together all the parts of society, and to restrain us from doing violence lest we be violently dealt withal ourselves.

The other part of justice is commonly called distributive, and is commanded in this rule, 'Render to all their dues: tribute to whom tribute is due: custom to whom custom; fear to whom fear; honour to whom honour. Owe no man anything, but to love one another'.[1]

This justice is distinguished from the first; because the obligation depends not upon contract or express bargain, but passes upon us by virtue of some command of God or of our superior, by nature or by grace, by piety or religion, by trust or by office, according to that commandment—'As every man hath received the gift, so let him minister the same, one to another as good stewards of the manifold grace of God'.[2] And as the first considers an equality of persons in respect of the contract or particular necessity, this supposes a difference of persons, and no particular bargains, but as by the laws of God or man are introduced. But I shall reduce all the particulars of both kinds to these four heads: obedience; provision; negotiation; restitution.

I OBEDIENCE

Our superiors are set over us in affairs of the world, or the affairs of the soul and things pertaining to religion, and are called accordingly ecclesiastical or civil. Our duty is described in the New Testament.

For temporal or civil governors the commands are these: 'Render to Caesar the things that are Caesar's'; and, 'Let every soul be subject to the higher powers: for there is no power but of God; the powers that be are ordained of God; whosoever, therefore, resisteth the power resisteth the ordinance of God; and they that resist shall receive to themselves damnation'[3]: and, 'Put them in mind to be subject to principalities and powers, and to obey magistrates'[4]: and, 'Submit yourselves to every ordinance of man, for the Lord's sake: whether it be to the king, as supreme; or unto governors, as unto them that are sent by Him for the punishment of evil doers, and the praise of them that do well'.[5]

For spiritual or ecclesiastical goverors, thus we are commanded: 'Obey them that have the rule over you, and submit yourselves; for they watch for your souls, as they that must give an account':[6] and 'Hold such in reputation'.[7] Our duty is reducible to practice by the following rules.

Acts and duties of obedience

1. We must obey all human laws appointed and constituted by lawful authority, that is, of the supreme power, according to the constitution of the place in which we live; all laws, I mean, which are not against the law of God.

2. In obedience to human laws, we must observe the letter of the law where we can, without doing violence to the reason of the law and the intention of the lawgiver; but where they cross each other, the charity of the law is to be preferred before its discipline, and the reason of it before the letter.

3. If the general reason of the law ceases in our particular, and a contrary reason rises upon us, we are to procure dispensation, or leave to omit the observance of it in such circumstances, if there be any persons or office appointed for granting it. If there be none, or if it is not easily to be had, or not without an inconvenience greater than the good of the observance of the law in our particular, we are dispensed withal in the nature of the thing without further process or trouble.

4. As long as the law is obligatory, so long our obedience is due; and he that begins a contrary custom without reason, sins; but he that breaks the law, when the custom is entered and fixed, is excused; because it is supposed the legislative power consents, when by not punishing it suffer disobedience to grow to up a custom.

5. Obedience to human laws must be for conscience sake; because public order, charity, and benefit is concerned, and because the law of God commands us. Next to the laws of God, we are to obey the laws of all our superiors, who, the more public they are, the first they are to be in the order of obedience.

6. Submit to the punishment and censure of the laws, and seek not to reverse their judgment by opposing, but by submitting, or flying, or silence, to pass through it or by it, as we can; and although from inferior judges we may appeal where the law permits us, yet we must sit down and rest in the judgment of the supreme; and if we be wronged, let us complain to God of the injury, not of the persons; and He will deliver thy soul from unrighteous judges.

7. Do not believe thou hast kept the law, when thou hast suffered

the punishment. The law punishes, not because she is as well pleased in taking vengeance as in being obeyed, but as a means to secure obedience for the future, or in others. Therefore, although the law is satisfied, yet the sins of irreligion, and scandal, and disobedience to God, must still be so accounted for, as to crave pardon and be washed off by repentance.

8. Human laws are not to be broken with scandal, nor at all without reason; for he that does it causelessly is a despiser of the law, and undervalues the authority. For human laws differ from divine laws principally in this: First, that the positive commands of a man may be broken upon smaller and more reasons than the positive commands of God; we may, upon a smaller reason, omit to keep any of the fasting-days of the Church than omit to give alms to the poor; a law, in a small matter, may be omitted for a small reason; in a great matter, not without a greater reason. And secondly the negative precepts of men may cease by contrary customs, public disrelish, long omission; but the negative precepts of God never can cease, but when they are expressly abrogated by the same authority. But what those reasons are that can dispense with the command of a man, a man may be his own judge; and a man shall walk most safely when he does not walk alone, but a spiritual man takes him by the hand.

9. We must not be too forward in procuring dispensations, nor use them any longer than the reason continues; for to be dispensed withal is an argument of natural infirmity, if it be necessary; but, if it be not, it signifies an undisciplined and unmortified spirit.

10. We must not be too busy in examining the prudence and unreasonableness of human laws: for although we are not bound to believe them all to be the wisest; yet, if we find them to fail of that wisdom with which some others are ordained, yet we must never make use of it to disparage the person of the lawgiver, or to countenance any man's disobedience, much less our own.

11. Pay that reverence to the person of thy prince, of his ministers, of thy parents and spiritual guides, which by the customs of the place thou livest in, are usually paid to such persons in their several degrees: expressed in all the circumstances and manners of the city and nation.

12. Lift not up thy hand against thy prince or parent, upon what pretence soever; but bear all personal affronts and inconveniences at their hands, and seek no remedy but by patience and piety, yielding and praying, or absenting thyself.

13. Speak not evil of the ruler of thy people, neither curse thy father or mother, nor revile thy spiritual guides, nor discover and lay naked their infirmities; but preserve their authority sacred by esteeming their persons venerable.

14. Pay tribute and customs to princes according to the laws, and maintenance to thy parents according to their necessity, and honourable support to the clergy according to the dignity of the work, and the customs of the place.

15. The good government of a king and of parents are actions of religion, as they relate to God, and of piety, as they relate to their people and families. For as he is not called a just father that educates his children well, but pious; so that prince who defends and well rules his people is religious, and does that duty for which alone he is answerable to God. If the prince or parent fail of their duty, we must not fail of ours; for we are answerable to them and to God too, as being accountable to all our superiors, and so are they to theirs: they are above us, and God is above them.

Remedies against disobedience, and means to endear our obedience

1. Consider that all authority descends from God, And this was St. Paul's argument for our obedience: 'The powers that be are ordained of God'.

2. There is very great peace and immunity from sin in resigning our wills up to the command of others: provided that our duty to God be secured. For since naturally we desire what is forbidden us (and sometimes there is no other evil in the thing but that it is forbidden us), God hath in grace enjoined and proportionably accepts obedience, and it is acceptable, although there be no other good in the thing that is commanded us, but that it is commanded.

3. By obedience we are made a society and a republic, and distinguished from herds of beasts, and heaps of flies, who do what they list, and are incapable of laws, and obey none; and therefore are killed and

destroyed, though never punished, and they never can have a reward.

4. By obedience we are rendered capable of all the blessings of government. He that ever felt, or saw, or can understand, the miseries of confusion in public affairs, or amazement in a heap of sad, tumultuous, and indefinite thoughts, may from thence judge of the admirable effects of order, and the beauty of government. What health is to the body, and peace is to the spirit, that is government to the societies of men; the greatest blessing which they can receive in that temporal capacity.

5. No man shall ever be fit to govern others that knows not first how to obey. For if the spirit of a subject be rebellious, in a prince it will be tyrannical and intolerable; and of so ill example, that as it will encourage the disobedience of others, so it will render it unreasonable for him to exact of others what in the like case he refused to pay.

6. There is no sin in the world which God hath punished with so great severity and high detestation, as this of disobedience.

7. He serves God better that follows his prince in lawful services than he that refuses his command upon pretence he must go say his prayers. But rebellion is compared to that sin which of all sin seems the most unnatural and damned impiety; 'Rebellion is as the sin of witchcraft'.

8. Obedience is a complicated act of virtue, and many graces are exercised in one act of obedience. It is an act of humility, of mortification and self-denial, of charity to God, of care of the public, of order and charity to ourselves and all our society, and a great instance of a victory over the most refractory and unruly passions.

9. To be a subject is a greater temporal felicity than to be a king: for all governments, have a great burden, huge care, infinite business, little rest, innumerable fears; and all that he enjoys above another is, the things of the world with other circumstances and a bigger noise. He, therefore, is an ungrateful person that will by disobedience, put more thorns into the crown or mitre of his superior. Much better is the advice of St. Paul: 'Obey them that have the rule over you, as they that must give an account for your souls; that they may do it with joy and not with grief: for,' (besides that is is unpleasant to them) 'it is unprofitable for you'.

10. All the wise men and all the good men of the world are obedient to their governors; and the eternal Son of God esteemed it His 'meat and drink to do the will of His Father'. No man ever came to perfection, but by obedience: and thousands of saints have chosen such institutions and manners of living in which they might not choose their own work, nor follow their own will, but be accountable to others, and subject to discipline, and obedient; as knowing this to be the highway of the cross, the way that the King of sufferings and humility did choose, and so became the King of glory.

11. No man ever perished who followed first the will of God, and then of his superiors: but thousands for following their own will, and relying upon their own judgments and choosing their own work, and doing their own fancies. For if we begin with ourselves, whatsoever seems good in our eyes is most commonly displeasing in the eyes of God.

12. Rebellion, though it be a spiritual sin, is of that disorder, unreasonableness, and impossiblity, amongst intelligent spirits, that they never murmured or mutinied against their superiors.

But because our superiors rule by their example, by their word or law, and by the rod, there are several degrees and parts of obedience, of several excellences and degrees towards perfection.

Degrees of obedience
The first is the obedience of our outward work: for because man cannot judge the heart, the public end is served, not by good wishes, but by real and actual performances; and if a man obeys against his will, he is not punishable by the laws.

Secondly, the obedience of the will: and this is also necessary in our obedience to human laws. For we are to do it as to the Lord, and not to men; and therefore we must do it willingly. But by this means our obedience in private is secured against secret arts and subterfuges: and we shall not decline our duty, but serve man for God's sake, that is, cheerfully, promptly, vigorously; for these are the proper parts of willingness and choice.

Thirdly, the understanding must yield obedience in general. We be not bound, in all cases, to think the particular law to be most prudent. But our rule is plain enough, Our understanding ought to be inquisitive, whether the civil constitution agree with our duty to God; but we are bound to inquire no further. Although he who enquires not at all into the wisdom or reasonableness of the law be not always the wisest man, yet he is ever the best subject provided that his duty to God be secured, he hath also, with the best and with all the instruments in the world, secured his obedience to man.

II JUSTICE

As God hath imprinted His authority upon several estates of men, as princes, parents, spiritual guides; so they may be instrumental in the conveying those blessings which God knows we need, and which should be the effects of government. They who have portions of these dignities have also their share of the administration; the sum of all which is in these two words, 'governing' and 'feeding', and is particularly recited in these following rules.

The duties of Kings, as lawgivers

1. Princes of the people, and all that have legislative power, must provide useful and good laws for the defence of propriety, for the encouragement of labour, for the safeguard of their persons, for determining controversies, for reward of noble actions and excellent arts and rare inventions, for promoting trade, and enriching their people.

2. In the making laws, princes must have regard to the public dispositions, to the affections and disaffections of the people, and must not introduce a law with public scandal and displeasure: but consider the public benefit, and the present capacity of affairs, and general inclinations of men's minds. For he that enforces a law upon a people against their first and public apprehensions, tempts them to disobedience, and to multiply their mutiny and their sin.

3. Princes must provide that the laws be duly executed, for a good law without execution is like an unperformed promise; and therefore they must be severe exactors of accounts from their delegates and ministers of justice.

4. The severity of laws must be tempered with dispensations,

pardons and remissions, according as the case shall alter.

5. Princes must be fathers of the people, and provide such instances of gentleness, ease, wealth, and advantages, as may make mutal confidence between them; and must fix their security, under God, in the love of the people; which, therefore they must with all arts of sweetness, remission, popularity, nobleness, and sincerity, endeavour to secure to themselves.

6. Princes must not multiply public oaths without great, eminent, and violent necessity; lest the security of the king become a snare to the people, and they become false, when they see themselves suspected; and if security of kings can be obtained otherwise, it is better that oaths should be the last refuge.

7. Let not the people be tempted with arguments to disobey, by the imposition of great and unnecessary taxes.

8. Princes must, in a special manner, be guardians of pupils and widows; by just laws, provident judges, and good guardians, ever having an ear ready open to their just complaints, and a heart full of pity, and one hand to support them, and the other to avenge them.

9. Princes must provide that the laws may be so administered that they be truly and really an ease to the people, not an instrument of vexation: and therefore must be careful that the shortest and most equal ways of trials be appointed, fees moderated, and intricacies and windings as much cut off as may be, lest injured persons be forced to perish under the oppression or under the law, in the injury, or in the suit. Laws are like princes, those best and most beloved who are most easy of access.

10. Places of judicature ought at no hand to be sold. For they that buy the office will sell the act; and they that at any rate will be judges, will not at any easy rate do justice; and their bribery is less punishable, when bribery opened the door by which they entered.

11. Ancient privileges, favours, customs, and acts of grace, indulged by former kings to their people, must not without high reason and great necessities, be revoked by their successors, nor laws be multiplied without great need; nor anything that may increase murmurs and lessen charity; always remembering that the interest of the prince and the people is so enfolded in a mutual embrace that

they cannot be untwisted without pulling a limb off, or dissolving the bands and conjunction of the whole body.

1 2. All princes must esteem themselves as much bound by their word as the meanest of their subjects are by the restraint and penalty of laws: and although they are superior to the people, yet they are not superior to their own engagements, their promises and oaths, when once they are passed from them.

The duty of judges

1. Judges must judge the causes of all persons uprightly and impartially, without any personal consideration of the power of the mighty, or the bribe of the rich, or the needs of the poor. The poor must fare no worse for his poverty, yet in justice he must fare no better for it: the rich must be no more regarded, yet he must not be less. The tutor of Cyrus instructed him, when in a controversy where a great boy would have taken a large coat from a little boy, because his own was to little for him and the other's was too big, he adjudged the great coat to the great boy: his tutor answered, 'Sir, if you were made a judge of decency or fitness, you had judged well in giving the biggest to the biggest; but when you are appointed judge, not whom the coat did fit, but whose it was, you should have considered the title and the possession, who did the violence, and who made it, or who bought it'. And so it must be in judgments between the rich and the poor; it is not to be considered what the poor man needs, but what is his own.

2. A prince may not, much less may inferior judges, deny justice, when it is legally and competently demanded: and if the prince will use his prerogative in pardoning an offender, he must be careful to give satisfaction to the injured person, and be watchful lest such indulgence might make persons more bold to do injury.

The duty of parents to their children

1. 'Fathers, provoke not your children to wrath'[8]: that is, be tender, pitiful, and gentle, complying with all the infirmities of the children, and in their several ages, according to their needs and their capacities.

2. 'Bring them up in the nurture and admonition of the Lord': that

is, secure their religion; season their younger years with prudent and pious principles; make them in love with virtue; and make them habitually so, before they come to choose or to discern good from evil, that their choice may be with less difficulty and danger. For while they are under discipline, they suck in all that they are first taught, and believe infinitely. Provide for them wise, learned, and virtuous tutors, and good company and discipline, seasonable baptism, catechism, and confirmation. For it is great folly to heap up much wealth for our children, and not to take care concerning the children for whom we get it. It is as if a man should take more care about his shoe than about his foot.

3. Parents must show piety at home;[9] that is, they must give good example and reverend deportment in the face of their children; sweetness of conversation, affability, frequent admonitions, all significations of love and tenderness, care and watchfulness—must be expressed towards children, that they may look upon their parents as their friends and patrons, their defence and sanctuary, their treasure and their guide. Hither is to be reduced the nursing of children, which is the first and most natural and necessary instance of piety which mothers can show to their babes; a duty from which nothing will excuse, but a disability, sickness, danger, or public necessity.

4. Parents must provide for their own,[10] according to their condition, education, and employment: enabling them, by competent portions, or good trades, arts, or learning, to defend themselves against the chances of the world, that they may not be exposed to temptation, to beggary, or unworthy arts. This must be done without covetousness, without impatient and greedy desires of making them rich; yet it must be done with much care and great affection, with all reasonable provision, and according to our power: and if we can, without sin, improve our estates for them, that also is part of the duty we owe to God for them. And this rule is to extend to all that descend from us, although we have been overtaken in a fault, and have unlawful issue; they also become part of our care, yet so as not to injure the production of the lawful bed.

5. This duty is to extend to a provision of conditions and an estate of life. Parents must, according to their power and reason,

provide husbands or wives for their children. In which they must
secure piety and religion, and the affection and love of the interested
persons: ever remembering that they can do no injury more afflictive
to the children than to join them with cords of a disagreeing affection; it is like tying a wolf and a lamb, or planting the vine in a
garden of coleworts. Let them be persuaded with reasonable induce-
ment to make them willing, and to choose according to the parent's
wish; but at no hand let them be forced.[11] Better to sit up all night
than to go to bed with a dragon.

Rules for married persons

1. Husbands must give to their wives love, maintenance, duty, and
the sweetness of conversation; and wives must pay to them all they
have or can, with the interest of obedience and reverence: and they
must be complicated in affections and interest, that there be no
distinction between them of 'mine' and 'thine'. And if the title be the
man's or the woman's, yet the use must be common; only the
wisdom of the man is to regulate all extravagances and indiscretions.
In other things no question is to be made; and their goods should be
as their children, not to be divided, but of one possession and provision: whatsoever is otherwise is not marriage but merchandise.
And upon this ground I suppose it was, that St. Basil commended that
woman who took part of her husband's goods to do good works
withal: for supposing him to be unwilling, and that the work was his
duty or hers alone, or both theirs in conjunction, or of great advantage to either of their souls, and no violence to the support of their
families, she had right to all that. As the humours of the body are
mingled with each other, so marriage may be a mixture of interests,
of bodies, of minds, of friends, a conjunction of the whole life, and
the noblest of friendships. But if, after all the fair deportments and
innocent chaste compliances, the husband be morose and ungentle,
let the wife discourse thus: 'If while I do my duty, my husband
neglects me, what will he do if I neglect him'? And if she thinks to be
separated by reason of her husband's unchaste life, let her consider,
that then the man will be incurably ruined, and her rivals could wish
nothing more than that they might possess him alone.

The duty of masters of families

1. The same care is to extend to all of our family, in their proportions, as to our children: for as, by St. Paul's economy, the heir differs nothing from a servant while he is in minority, so a servant should differ nothing from a child, in the substantial part of the care; and the difference is only in degrees. Servants and masters are of the same kindred, of the same nature, and heirs of the same promises and therefore, first, must be provided of necessaries, for their support and maintenance; secondly, they must be used with mercy; thirdly, their work must be tolerable and merciful; fourthly, their restraints must be reasonable; fifthly, their recreations fitting and healthful; sixthly, their religion and the interest of souls taken care of; and seventhly, masters must correct their servants with gentleness, prudence, and mercy; not for every slight fault, not always, not with upbraiding and disgraceful language, but with such only as may express and reprove the fault, and amend the person. But in all these things measures are to be taken by the contract made, by the laws and customs of the place. No servant will do his duty, unless he make a conscience, or love his master: if he does it not for God's sake or his master's, he will not need to do it always for his own.

The duty of guardians or tutors

Tutors and Guardians are in the place of parents; and what they are in fiction of law, they must remember to do in reality of duty.

(Note—The duty of ministers and spiritual guides to the people is of so great burden, so various rules, so intricate and busy caution, that it requires a distinct tractate by itself).

III NEGOTIATION, OR CIVIL CONTRACTS

This part of justice depends upon the laws of man directly, and upon the laws of God only by consequence and indirect reason; and our duty is plain and easy, requiring of us honesty in contracts, sincerity in affirming, simplicity in bargaining, and faithfulness in performing.

Rules and measures of justice in bargaining

1. In making contracts, use not many words; he that speaks least means fairest, as having fewer opportunities to deceive.

2. Lie not at all, neither in a little thing nor in a great, neither in the substance nor in the circumstance, neither in word nor deed: that is, pretend not what is false, cover not what is true; and let the measure of your affirmation or denial be the understanding of your contractor; for he that deceives the buyer or the seller by speaking what is true in a sense not intended or understood by the other, is a liar and a thief. For in bargains you are to avoid not only what is false, but that also which deceives.

3. In prices of bargaining concerning uncertain merchandises, you may buy as cheap ordinarily as you can; and sell as dear as you can, so it be, first, without violence; and secondly, when you contract on equal terms with persons in all senses (as to the matter and skill of bargaining) equal to yourself, that is, merchants with merchants, wise men with wise men, rich with rich; and thirdly, when there is no deceit, and no necessity, and no monopoly; both parties are voluntary, and therefore there can be no injustice or wrong to either. Add also this consideration, that the public be not oppressed by unreasonable and unjust rates: for which the following rules are the best measure.

4. Let your prices be according to that measure of good and evil which is established in the fame and common accounts of the wisest and most merciful men, skilled in that manufacture or commodity; and the gain such as which without scandal be allowed to persons in all the same circumstances.

5. Let no prices be heightened by the necessity or unskilfulness of the contractor: for the first is direct uncharitableness to the person, and injustice in the thing; because the man's necessity could not naturally enter into the consideration of the value of the commodity; and the other is deceit and oppression. Much less must any man make necessities; as by engrossing a commodity, by monopoly, by detaining corn, or the like indirect arts; for such persons are unjust to all single persons with whom they contract, and oppressors of the public.

6. Keep something within thy power. There is a latitude of gain in buying and selling; take not thou the utmost penny for although it be lawful, yet it is not safe; and he that gains all that he can gain lawfully this year, possibly next year will be tempted to gain something unlawfully.

7. He that sells dearer, by reason he sells not for ready money, must increase his price no higher than to make himself recompense for the loss which he sustained by his forbearance, reckoning in also the hazard, which he is prudently, warily, and charitably, to estimate. But although this be the measure of his justice, yet because it happens either to their friends, or to necessitous and poor persons, they are in these cases, to consider the rules of friendship and neighbourhood, and the obligations of charity, lest justice turn into unmercifulness.

8. No man is to be raised in his price or rents in regard of any accident, advantage, or disadvantage, of his person.

9. Let no man, for his own poverty, become more oppressing and cruel in his bargain, but quietly, modestly, diligently, and patiently, recommend his estate to God, and, if they cure not his poverty, they will take away the evil of it: and there is nothing else in it that can trouble him.

10. Detain not the wages of the hireling; it is injustice and uncharitableness, but pay him exactly according to covenant, or according to his needs.

11. Religiously keep all promises and covenants, though made to your disadvantage, though afterwards you perceive you might have been better. Let nothing make you break your promise, unless it be unlawful, or impossible; either out of your natural, or out of your civil power, yourself being under the power of another; or that it be intolerably inconvenient to yourself, and of no advantage to another; or that you have leave expressed, or reasonably presumed.

12. Let no man take wages or fees for a work that he cannot do, or cannot with probability undertake, and with ease, or with advantage manage. Physicians must not meddle with desperate diseases, and known to be incurable, without declaring their sense beforehand; that if the patient please, he may entertain him at adventure, or to do

him some little ease. Advocates must deal plainly with their clients, and tell them the true state and danger of their case; and must not pretend confidence in an evil cause.

1 3. Let no man appropriate to his own use what God, or the republic, hath made common; for that is both against justice and charity too.

IV RESTITUTION

Restitution is that part of justice to which a man is obliged by a precedent contract or a foregoing fault, by his own act or another man's, either with or without his will. He that borrows is bound to pay, and much more he that steals or cheats. For in all sins we are to distinguish the transient or passing act from the remaining effect or evil. The act of stealing was soon over, and cannot be undone; and for it the sinner is to expiate it by suffering punishment, and repenting, and asking pardon, doing acts of justice and charity, in contradiction to that evil action. But because, in stealing, there is an injury done to our neighbour, and the evil still remains after the action is past; for this we are accountable to our neighbour. Upon this ground, it is a determined rule in divinity, 'Our sin can never be pardoned, till we have restored what we unjustly took': restored it (I mean) actually, or in purpose and desire. The practice of this part of justice is to be directed by the following rules.

Rules of making restitution

1. Whosoever is an effective real cause of doing his neighbour wrong, by what instrument soever he does it, is bound to make restitution to his neighbour; if without him the injury had not been done, but by him or his assistance, it was.

2. He that commanded the injury to be done, is first bound: then he that did it; and after these, they also are obliged who did so assist. If satisfaction be made by any of the former, the latter is tied to repentance, but no restitution: but if the injured person be not righted, every one of them is wholly guilty of the injustice; and therefore bound to restitution, singly and entirely.

3. Whosoever intends a little injury to his neighbour, and acts it, and by it a greater evil accidentally comes, he is obliged to make an entire reparation. He that set fire on a plane-tree to spite his neighbour, and the plane-tree set fire on his neighbour's house, is bound to pay for all the loss, because it did all rise from his own ill intention.

4. He that hinders a charitable person from giving alms to a poor man, is tied to restitution if he hindered him by fraud or violence, because it was a right which the poor man had. But if the alms were hindered only by entreaty, the hinderer is not tied to restitution, because entreaty took not liberty away from the giver, but left him still master of his own act, and he had power to alter his purpose, and so long there was no injustice done. The same is the case of a testator giving a legacy. He that hinders the charitable legacy by fraud or violence is equally obliged to restitution.

5. He that refuses to do any part of his duty to which he is otherwise obliged, without a bribe, is bound to restore that money, because he took it in his neighbour's wrong, and not as a salary for his labour, or a reward for his wisdom.

6. He that takes anything from his neighbour which was justly forfeited, is tied to repentance, but not to restitution. For my neighbour is not the worse for my act, but because I took the forfeiture indirectly I am answerable to God for my unhandsome, unjust, or uncharitable circumstances.

7. The heir is not bound to make restitution if the obligation passed only by a personal act; but if it passed from his person to his estate, then the estate passes with all its burden.

8. He that by fact, or word, or sign, either fraudulently or violently, does hurt to his neighbour's body, life, goods, good name, friends, or soul, is bound to make restitution capable to be made. We must separate entreaty and enticements from deceit or violence. If I persuade my neighbour to commit adultery, I still leave him or her in their own power; and though I am answerable to God for my sin, yet not to my neighbour. For I made her to be willing, yet she was willing, that is, the same at last as I was at first. But if I have used fraud, and made her to believe a lie, upon which confidence she did the act, and without she would not (as if I tell a woman her husband

is dead, or intended to kill her, or is himself an adulterous man), or if I use violence or anything that takes her from the liberty of her choice, I am bound to restitution; that is, to restore her to a right understanding of things and to a full liberty, by taking from her the deceit or the violence.

9. An adulterous person is tied to restitution of the injury, so far as it is reparable; to make provision for the children begotten in unlawful embraces, that they may do no injury to the legitimate by receiving a common portion; and if the injured person do account of it, he must satisfy him with money for the wrong done to his bed. He is not tied to offer this, because it is no proper exchange, but he is bound to pay it if it be reasonably demanded; for every man hath justice done him when himself is satisfied, though by a word, or an action, or a penny.

10. He that hath killed a man is bound to restitution, by allowing such a maintenance to the children and near relatives of the deceased, as they have lost by his death, considering and allowing for all circumstances of the man's age, and health, and probability of living.

11. He that hath really lessened the fame of his neighbour by fraud or violence is bound to restore it by confession of his fault, giving testimony of its innocence or worth, doing him honour, or by money, which answers all things.

12. He that hath wounded his neighbour is tied to the expenses of the surgeon and other incidences, and to repair whatever loss he sustains by his disability to work or trade. Thus a ravisher must repair the temporal detriment or injury done to the maid, and give her a dowry, or marry her if she desire it. For this restores her into that capacity of being a good wife, as far as it can be done.

13. He that robbeth his neighbour is bound not only to restore the principal but all emoluments during the time of their being detained. By these rules we may judge of the obligation that lies upon all sorts of injurious persons; the sacrilegious, cheaters of men's inheritances, unjust judges, false witnesses, and accusers; those that do fraudulently or violently bring men to sin, that force men to drink, that laugh at and disgrace virtue, that persuade servants to run away, violent persecutors of religion in any instance; and all of the same nature.

14. He that hath wronged so many as in daily trade, that he knows not in what measure he hath done it, must redeem his fault by alms and largesses to the poor, according to the value of his wrongful dealing, as near as he can proportion it. Better it is to go begging to heaven, than to go to hell laden with the spoils of rapine and injustice.

15. The order of paying the debts of contract or restitution are in some instances set down by the civil laws of a kingdom. In want of such rules, we are to observe first, the necessity of the creditor; then secondly, the time of the delay; and thirdly, the special obligations of friendship or kindness; and according to these, in their several degrees, make our restitution. Remember that the same day in which Zaccheus made restitution to all whom he had injured, the same day Christ Himself pronounced that salvation was come to his house.

16. But besides the obligation arising from contract or default, there is one of another sort which comes from kindness, and the acts of charity and friendship. The obligation comes not by covenant, but by the nature of the thing, and is a duty springing up within the spirit of the obliged person, to whom it is more natural to love his friend, and to do good for good, than to return evil for evil. A man may forgive an injury, but he must never forget a good turn. For everything that is excellent, and everything that is profitable, whatsoever is good in itself, or good to me, cannot but be beloved; and what we love we naturally cherish and do good to.

Prayers to be said in relation to the obligations and offices of justice

A Prayer for the grace of obedience

O eternal God, who hast constituted all things in a wonderful order, making all the creatures subject to man, and one man to another, and all to Thee, teach me to obey all those whom Thou hast set over me, cheerfully undergoing those burdens which the public wisdom and necessity shall impose upon me, at no hand murmuring against government, lest the spirit of pride and mutiny, of murmur and disorder, enter into me, and consign me to the portion of the disobedient and rebellious, of the despisers of dominion, and revilers of dignity. Grant this, for His sake who, for His obedience to the Father, hath obtained the glorification of eternal ages, our Lord and Saviour Jesus Christ. *Amen.*

A Prayer to be said by subjects

I

O eternal God, Thou alone rulest in the kingdoms of men; let the light of Thy countenance, and the effects of a glorious mercy and a gracious pardon, return to this land. Provide us of remedy against our present calamities; let not the defenders of a righteous cause go away ashamed, nor religion be suppressed, nor learning discountenanced, nor we be spoiled of the advantages of piety. *Amen.*

II

Lord, remember our infirmities, and no more remember our sins; support us with Thy staff, lift us up with Thy hand, refresh us with Thy gracious eye; and if a sad cloud of temporal infelicities must still encircle us, open unto us the window of heaven, that, with an eye of faith and hope, we may see beyond the cloud. Teach us diligently to do all our duty, and cheerfully to submit to all Thy will; and, at last, be gracious to Thy people that besides Thee have no helper. *Amen.*

A Prayer to be said by Kings or magistrates for themselves and their people

O God, by Thee Kings reign and princes decree justice; Thou hast appointed me under Thyself (and under my prince) to govern according to the laws of religion and the commonwealth, give to Thy servant an understanding heart to judge this people, that I may discern between good and evil. Cause me to walk in truth and righteousness, and in sincerity of heart, that doing justice to all men, I and my people may receive peace and plenty in our days; that there be no complaining in our streets, but we may see the Church in prosperity and religion established and increasing, for His sake, who is my Lord and King, our Redeemer, Jesus. *Amen.*

A Prayer to be said by parents for their children

O Almighty and most merciful Father, who hast given children to me as a testimony of Thy mercy, and an engagement of my duty; give them healthful bodies, understanding souls, and sanctified spirits, that they may be Thy servants and Thy children all their days. Lead them through the dangers, and temptations, and ignorances of their youth, that they may never run into folly and the evils of an unbridled appetite.

So order the accidents of their lives, that by good education, careful tutors, holy example, innocent company, prudent counsel, and thy restraining grace, their duty to thee may be secured in the midst of a crooked and untoward generation. Enable me to provide for the support of their persons, that they may not be destitute and miserable in my death. Let them glorify Thee here with a free obedience, that when they have served Thee in their generations, and have profited the Christian commonwealth, they may be coheirs in the glories of Thy eternal kingdom, through our Lord Jesus Christ. Amen.

A Prayer to be said by masters of families, curates, tutors, or other responsible persons, for their charges

O Almighty God, merciful and gracious, have mercy upon my family (or pupils or parishioners, etc.) and all committed to my charge; preserve them with Thy providence, guard them from all evil, direct them in the ways of peace and holy religion by my ministry and the conduct of Thy most Holy Spirit. Consign them with Thy blessings and graces in this world, with healthful bodies, good understandings and sanctified spirits, to a full fruition of Thy glories hereafter, through Jesus Christ our Lord. Amen.

A Prayer to be said by merchants, tradesmen, and handicraftsmen

O eternal God, Thou fountain of justice, mercy, and benediction, who by education hast called me to this profession, that by my industry, I may work together for the good of myself and others. Guide me in my intention, and in the transaction of my affairs, that I may be diligent, just, and faithful; that this my labour may be accepted as a part of my necessary duty; assist and prosper me, let thy Holy Spirit be for ever present with me, that I may never be given to covetousness and sordid appetites, to lying and falsehood, or any other base, indirect, and beggarly arts; but give me prudence, honesty, and Christian sincerity, that my trade may be sanctified by my religion, my labour by my intention and Thy blessing; that when I have done my portion of work alloted me, and improved the talent intrusted to me, and served the commonwealth in my capacity, I may receive the portion and inheritance of the ever-blessed Saviour and Redeemer, Jesus. Amen.

A Prayer to be said by debtors

O Almighty God, we being Thy debtors by reason of our sins, and by Jesus Christ; teach me to perform all my obligations to Thee, both of duty and thankfulness; enable me to pay my duty to all my friends, and my debts to all my creditors, that none be made miserable or lessened in his estate by his kindness or traffic with me. Forgive me all those sins and irregular actions by which I entered into debt further than my necessity required, let not them suffer by occasion of my sin. Lord, reward all their kindness and make me willing in all that I can, and able for all that I am obliged to; that the prayer of Thy servant may obtain of Thee, at least, to pay my debt in blessings. *Amen.*

NOTES: CHAPTER 3

1 Rom. XIII[7]
2 I Peter IV[10]
3 Rom. XIII[1, 2]
4 Titus III[1]
5 I Peter II[13, 14]
6 Heb. XIII[17]
7 Phil. II[29]
8 Ephes. VI[4]
9 Heb. XII[9] I Tim. V[4]
10 I Tim. V[8]
11 Gen. XXIV[57, 58]

4·Christian religion

Religion, in a large sense, doth signify the whole duty of man, comprehending in it justice, charity, and sobriety; because all these being commanded by God, they become a part of that honour and worship which we are bound to pay to Him. And thus the word is used in St. James, 'Pure religion and undefiled before God and the Father is this, to visit the fatherless and widows in their affliction, and to keep himself unspotted from the world'.[1] But, it particularly relates to God, in our worshippings and adoration of Him, in confessing His excellences, loving His person, admiring His goodness, believing His word, and doing all that which may do Him honour. So it is called godliness,[2] and is by St. Paul distinguished from justice and sobriety. In this sense I am now to explicate the parts of it.

The internal acts of religion
Those I call the internal actions of religion, in which the soul only is employed, and ministers to God in the special actions of faith, hope, and charity. Faith believes the revelations of God: hope expects His promises: and charity loves His excellences and mercies. Faith gives our understanding to God: hope gives up all the passions and affections to heaven and heavenly things: and charity gives the will to the service of God. Faith is opposed to infidelity, hope to despair,

charity to enmity and hostility: and these three sanctify the whole man, and make our duty to God and obedience to His commandments to be chosen, reasonable, and delightful, and therefore to be entire, persevering, and universal.

I FAITH

The acts and offices of faith are:

1. To believe everything which God hath revealed to us: and, when once we are convinced that God hath spoken it, to make no further inquiry, but humbly to submit, ever remembering that there are some things which our understanding cannot fathom, nor search out their depth.

2. Faith is the parent of charity; and whatsoever faith entertains must be apt to produce love to God: but he that believes God to be cruel or unmerciful, thinks evil thoughts concerning God, and such as for which we should hate a man, and therefore are great enemies of faith, being apt to destroy charity. In our discourses, we must remove from Him all imperfection, and attribute to Him all excellency.

3. To give ourselves wholly up to Christ, in heart and desire, to become disciples of His doctrine with choice (besides conviction), being in the presence of God but as idiots, that is, without any principles of our own to hinder the truth of God, believing it infinitely, and loving to believe it. For this is an act of love, reflected upon faith; or an act of faith, leaning upon love.

4. To believe all God's promises: this act makes us to rely upon God with the same confidence as we did on our parents when we were children, when we made no doubt but whatsoever we needed, we should have it, if it were in their power.

5. Many are apt to believe the article of remission of sins, but they believe it without the condition of repentance, or the fruits of holy life and this is otherwise than God intended it. For the covenant of the Gospel is the great object of faith, and that supposes our duty to answer His grace; that God will be our God, so long as we are His people. The other is not faith, but flattery.

6. To profess publicly Jesus Christ, openly owning whatsoever He

hath revealed and commanded, not being ashamed of the word of God: and not regarding favour, nor being moved with good words, not fearing disgrace, or loss, or inconvenience, or death itself.

7. To pray without doubting, without weariness, without faintness; entertaining no jealousies or suspicions of God, but being confident of God's hearing us.

These acts of faith are, in several degrees, in the servants of Jesus; some have it but as a grain of mustard seed; some grow up to a plant; some have the fulness of faith: but the least faith that is, must be a persuasion so strong as to make us undertake the doing of all that duty which Christ built upon the foundation of believing. But we shall best discern the truth of our faith by these following signs. St. Jerome reckons three.

Signs of true faith

1. An earnest and vehement prayer: for it is impossible we should heartily believe the things of God and the glories of the gospel, and not most importunately desire them. For everything is desired according to our belief of its excellency and possibility.

2. To do nothing for vainglory, but wholly for the interests of religion, and these articles we believe; valuing not at all the rumours of men, but the praise of God.

3. To be content with God for our judge, for our patron, for our Lord, for our friend; desiring God to be all in all to us, as we are, in our understanding and affections, wholly His.
Add to these:

4. To be a stranger upon earth in our affections, and to have all our thoughts and principal desires fixed upon the matters of faith, the things of heaven. For if a man were adopted heir to a king, he would (if he believed it real and effective) wholly be at court in his father's eye; and all his thoughts would spend themselves in creating ideas and fantastic images of his future condition. Now God hath made us heirs of His kingdom, and coheirs with Jesus: if we believed this, we should think, and affect, and study accordingly.

5. St. James's sign is the best: 'Shew me thy faith by thy works'. Faith makes the merchant diligent and venturous, and that makes him

rich. Ferdinand of Arragon believed the story told him by Columbus, and therefore he furnished him with ships, and got the West Indies by his faith in the undertaker; But Henry VII of England believed him not; and therefore trusted him not with shipping, and lost all the purchase of that faith. No man could work a day's labour without faith; but because he believes he shall have his wages at the day's or week's end, he does his duty. But he only believes who does that thing which other men in like cases do when they do believe. He that believes money gotten with danger is better than poverty with safety, will venture for it in unknown lands or seas; and so will he that believes it better to get heaven with labour, than to go to hell with pleasure.

6. He that believes waits patiently till the times of refreshment come, and dares trust God for the morrow. If you dare trust to God when the case, to human reason, seems impossible, and trust out of choice not because you have nothing else to trust to, then you give a good testimony of your faith.

7. True faith is confident, and will venture all the world upon the strength of its persuasion. Will you lay your life on it, your estate, your reputation, that the doctrine of Jesus Christ is true in every article? Then you have true faith. But he that fears men more than God, believes men more than he believes in God.

8. Faith, if it be true, living, and justifying, cannot be separated from a good life; it works miracles, makes a drunkard become sober, a lascivious person become chaste, a covetous man become liberal; it 'overcomes the world', it 'works righteousness'[3] and makes us diligently to do, and cheerfully to suffer, whatsover God hath placed in our way to heaven.

The means to obtain faith are:

1. A humble, willing mind, or desire to be instructed in the way of God; for persuasion enters like a sunbeam, gently, and without violence; and open but the window, and draw the curtain, and the Sun of righteousness will enlighten your darkness.

2. An unchaste man cannot easily be brought to believe that, without purity, he shall never see God. He that loves riches can hardly

believe the doctrine of poverty and renunciation of the world. He that hath within him any principle contrary to the doctrines of faith cannot easily become a disciple.

3. Prayer, which is instrumental to everything, hath a particular promise in this. 'He that lacks wisdom, let him ask it of God': and, 'If you give good things to your children, how much more shall your heavenly Father give His Spirit to them that ask Him?'

4. The consideration of the divine omnipotence and infinite wisdom, and our own ignorance, are great instruments of curing all doubting, and silencing the murmurs of infidelity.

5. True faith is full of ingenuity and simplicity, free from suspicion wise and confident, trusting without watching and prying into indiscernible particulars. No man carries his bed into his field, to watch how his corn grows, but believes upon the general order of providence and nature; and at harvest finds himself not deceived.

6. In time of temptation, be not busy to dispute, but throw yourself upon God: in prayer, and in the presence and with the help of a prudent untempted guide; and be sure to esteem all changes of belief which offer themselves in the time of your greatest weakness to be temptations, and reject them accordingly.

7. In health, lay up particular arguments and instruments of persuasion and confidence, especially in those things in which we be most tempted, and are least confident, and which commonly the devil uses to assault us.

8. The wisdom of the Church of God is very remarkable in appointing festivals or holy days to record the article of the day; such as Trinity Sunday, Ascension, Easter, Christmas-day; and to those persons who can only believe, not prove or dispute, there is no better instrument to cause the remembrance, and to endear the affection and hearty assent to the article, than the proclaiming and recommending it by the festivity and joy of a holy day.

II THE HOPE OF A CHRISTIAN

Faith is of all things revealed, good and bad, rewards and punishments, of things past, present, and to come; but hope hath for its object things only that are good, and fit to be hoped for, future, and concerning ourselves; and because these things are offered to us upon conditions of which we may so fail, as we may change our will, therefore our certainty is less than the adherences of faith. For it is infallibly certain that there is heaven for all the godly, and for me amongst them all, if I do my duty. But that I shall enter into heaven is the object of my hope, not of my faith; and is so sure, as it is certain I shall persevere in the ways of God.

The acts of hope are:

1. To rely upon God with a confident expectation of His promises.

2. To esteem all the danger of an action, and the possibilities of miscarriage to be no defect on God's part, but either a mercy on His part, or a fault on ours. The hope of a Christian is prudent and religious.

3. To rejoice in the midst of a misfortune or seeming sadness, knowing that this may work for good, and will, if we be not wanting to our souls. This is a direct act of hope to look through the cloud, and look for a beam of the light from God; and is called in Scripture 'rejoicing in tribulation', when 'the God of hope fills us with all joy in believing'. Every degree of hope brings a degree of joy.

4. To desire, to pray and to long for the great object of our hope, God's glory and the great end of our souls. Hope and fasting are said to be the two wings of prayer. Fasting is but as the wing of a bird; but hope is like the wing of an angel, soaring up to heaven, and bears our prayers to the throne of grace. Without hope, it is impossible to pray; but hope makes our prayers reasonable, passionate, and religious; for it relies upon God's promise, or experience, or providence. Prayer is always in proportion to our hope, zealous and affectionate.

5. Perseverance is the perfection of the duty of hope, and its last act; and so long as our hope continues, so long we go on in duty and diligence; but he that is to raise a castle in an hour, sits down and does nothing towards it.

Rules to govern our hope

1. Let hope be moderate; proportioned to your state, person, and

condition, whether it be for gifts or graces, or temporal favours. A
stammerer cannot, with moderation, hope for the gift of tongues; or
a peasant to become learned as Origen. Hope for good success
according to, or not much beyond, the efficacy of the causes and the
instrument; and let the husbandman hope for a good harvest, not for
a rich kingdom, or a victorious army.

2. Let your hope be well founded, that is, upon God, according to
His revelations and promises. It is presumption to hope that God's
mercies will be poured forth upon lazy persons, that do nothing towards holy and strict walking, nothing (I say) but trust and long for
an event besides and against all disposition of the means. Rely not in
temporal things upon uncertain prophecies and astrology, not upon
our own wit or industry, not upon gold or friends, not upon armies
and princes; expect not health from physicians, that cannot cure their
own breath, much less their mortality: use all lawful instruments, but
expect nothing from them above their natural or ordinary efficacy,
and, in the use of them, from God expect a blessing. A hope that is
easy and credulous is an arm of flesh, an ill supporter without a bone.

3. Let your hope be without vanity, or garishness of spirit; but
sober, grave, and silent, fixed in the heart, not borne upon the lip,
apt to support our spirits within, but not to provoke envy abroad.

4. Let your hope be of things possible, safe, and useful. He that
hopes for an opportunity of acting his revenge, or lust, or rapine,
watches to do himself a mischief. All evils of ourselves or brethren
are objects of our fear, not hope; and when truly understood, things
useless and unsafe can no more be wished for than things impossible
can be obtained.

5. Let your hope be patient. Make no limits or prescriptions to
God, and take not every accident for an argument of despair; but go
on still in hoping; and begin again to work if any ill accident have
interrupted you.

Means of hope, and remedies against despair
The means to cure despair, and to continue or increase hope, are
partly by consideration, partly by exercise.

1. Apply your mind to the cure of all the proper causes of despair;

and they are, weakness of spirit or violence of passion. He that greedily covets is impatient of delay and desperate in contrary accidents; and he that is little of heart is also little of hope, and apt to sorrow and suspicion.

2. Where there is less variety of chance, there is less possibility of being mocked: but he that creates to himself thousands of little hopes, uncertain in the promise, fallible in the event, and depending upon ten thousand circumstances (as are all the things of this world), shall often fail in his expectations.

3. So long as your hopes are regular and reasonable, such as are deliverance from enemies, escaping a storm or shipwreck, recovery from a sickness, ability to pay your debts, etc., remember that there are some things ordinary, and some things extraordinary, to prevent despair. In ordinary, remember that the very hoping in God is an endearment of Him, and a means to obtain the blessing; 'I will deliver him, because he hath put his trust in Me'. Secondly, there are in God all those glorious attributes and excellences which in the nature of things can possibly create or confirm hope: God is strong, wise, true, loving. Upon these premises we cannot fail of receiving what is fit for us. Thirdly, God hath obliged Himself by promise, that we shall have the good of everything we desire: for even losses and denials shall work for the good of them that fear God. And if we will trust the truth of God for performance of the general, we may well trust His wisdom to choose for us the particular. But the extraordinaries of God are apt to supply the defect of all natural and human possibilities. God hath, in many instances, given extraordinary virtue to the active causes and instruments— to a jawbone, to kill a multitude; to three hundred men, to destroy a great army; to Jonathan and his armourbearer, to rout a whole garrison. He hath given excellent sufferance and vigorousness to the sufferers, arming them with strange courage, heroical fortitude, invincible resolution, and glorious patience: and thus He lays no more upon us than we are able to bear, for when He increases our sufferings, He lessens them by increasing our patience. His providence produces strange things beyond common rules; He led Israel through a sea, and made a rock pour forth waters, and the heavens to give them bread and flesh, and whole armies to be

destroyed with fantastic noises, and the fortune of all France to be recovered and entirely revolved by the arms and conduct of a girl, against the torrent of the English fortune and chivalry. And it is impossible for that man to despair who remembers that his helper is omnipotent, and can do what He please.[4] Let us rest there a while; He can if He please: and He is infinitely loving, willing enough; and He is infinitely wise, choosing better for us than we can do for ourselves. This in all ages hath supported the afflicted people of God: God invites and cherishes the hopes of men.

4. If your case be brought to the last extremity, at the pit's brink, even the very margin of the grave, yet then despair not. Remember that whatsoever final accident takes away all hope from you, bear it sweetly, it will also take away all despair too. For when you enter into the regions of death you rest from all your labours and your fears.

5. Let them who are tempted to despair consider how much Christ suffered to redeem us from sin, and he must needs believe that the desires which God had to save us were not less than infinite.

6. Let no man despair of God's mercies to forgive him, unless he be sure that his sins are greater than God's mercies.

7. Consider that God, who knows all the events of men, calls them to be His own, gives them blessings, arguments of mercy and instances of fear to call them off from death, and to call them home to life; and in all this shows no despair of happiness to them; and therefore much less should any man despair for himself.

8. Remember that despair belongs only to passionate fools or villains such as were Achitopel and Judas, or to devils and damned persons; and as the hope of salvation is a good disposition towards it, so is despair a certain consignation to eternal ruin. A man may be damned for despairing to be saved. Despair is the proper passion of damnation. 'God hath placed truth and felicity in heaven, curiosity and repentance upon earth, but misery and despair are the portions of hell'. (Venerable Bede).

9. Gather together into your spirit, and its treasure-house the memory, not only all the promises of God, but also the remembrances of experience, and the former senses of the divine favours, that from

thence you may argue from times past to the present, and enlarge to the future and to greater blessings. For although the conjectures and expectations of hope are not like the conclusions of faith, yet they are a helmet against the scorchings of despair in temporal things, and an anchor of the soul sure and steadfast, against the fluctuations of the spirit in matters of the soul. St. Bernard reduces to these three the instruments of all our hopes: First, the charity of God adopting us; secondly, the truth of His promises; thirdly, the power of His performance. This was St. Paul's instrument: 'Experience begets hope, and hope maketh not ashamed'.

10. Do thou take care only of thy duty, of the means and proper instruments of thy purpose, and leave the end to God: lay that up with Him, and He will take care of all that is intrusted to Him: and this, being an act of confidence in God, is also a means of security to thee.

11. Secure the confident belief of the resurrection; and thou canst not but hope for everything else which you may reasonably expect, or lawfully desire, upon the stock of the divine mercies and promises.

12. If a despair seizes you in a particular temporal instance, let it not defile thy spirit, or mingle in spiritual considerations; but rather let it make thee fortify thy soul, that by being thrown out of your earthly confidence, you may retire into the strengths of grace, that despair become the necessity of all virtue.

III CHARITY, OR THE LOVE OF GOD

Love is the greatest thing that God can give us; for Himself is love: and it is the greatest thing we can give to God; for it will also give ourselves, and carry with it all that is ours. The apostle calls it the band of perfection; it is the old, and it is the new, and it is the great commandment; and it is all the commandments; for it is the fulfilling of the law. It does the work of all other graces without any instrument but its own immediate virtue. For as the love to sin makes a man sin against all his own reason, and all the discourses of wisdom, and all the advices of his friends, and without temptation, and without opportunity; so does the love of God; it makes a man chaste without the laborious arts of fasting and exterior disciplines, temperate in the midst of feasts, and is active enough to choose it without any intermedial appetites, and reaches at glory through the very heart of grace, without any other arms but those of love. It is a grace that loves God for Himself, and our neighbours for God. The consideration of God's goodness and bounty, the experience of those profitable and excellent emanations from Him, may be, and most commonly are, the first motive of our love; but when we are once entered, and have tasted the goodness of God, we love the spring for its own excellency, passing from passion to reason, from thanking to adoring, from sense to spirit, from considering ourselves to a union with God: and this is the image and little representation of heaven; it is beatitude in picture, or rather the infancy and beginnings of glory.

We need no incentives to move us to the love of God; for we cannot love anything for any reason real or imaginary. There can but two things create love— perfection and usefulness: to which answer on our part, first, admiration; and secondly, desire; and both these are centred in love. For the entertainment of the first, there is in God an infinite nature, immensity or vastness without extension or limit, immutability, eternity, omnipotence, omniscience, holiness, dominion, providence, bounty, mercy, justice, perfection in Himself, and the end to which all things and all actions must be directed, and will at last arrive. Consider our distance from all these glories; our smallness and limited nature, our nothing, our inconstancy, our age like a span, our weakness and ignorance, our poverty, our inadvertency and inconsideration, our disabilities and disaffections to do good, our harsh natures and unmerciful inclinations, our universal iniquity, and our necessities and dependencies, not only on God originally and essentially, but even our need of the meanest of God's creatures, and our being obnoxious to the weakest and most contemptible. But, for the entertainment of the second, we may consider that in Him is a torrent of pleasure for the voluptuous; He is the fountain of honour for the ambitious, an inexhaustible treasure for the covetous. Our vices are in love with fantastic pleasures and images of perfection, which are truly and really to be found nowhere but in God. And therefore our virtues have such proper objects that it is but reasonable they should all turn into love; for certain it is that this love will turn all into virtue. For in the scrutinies for righteousness and judgment, when it is inquired whether such a person be a good man or no, the meaning is not, What does he believe? or what does he hope? but what he loves.

The acts of love to God are:
1. Love does all things which may please the beloved person; it performs all his commandments: and this is one of the greatest instances and arguments of our love that God requires of us—'this is love, that we keep His commandments': love is obedient.
2. It does all the intimations and secret significations of his pleasure whom we love; and this is an argument of a great degree of it. The first instance is, it makes the love accepted: but this gives a greatness and singularity to it. The first is the least, and less than it cannot do our duty; but without this second we cannot come to perfection. Great love is also pliant and inquisitive in the instances of its expression.
3. Love gives away all things, that so he may advance the interest of the beloved person: it relieves all that he would have relieved, and spends itself in such real significations as it is enabled withal. He never loved God that will quit anything of his religion to save his money: love is always liberal and communicative.
4. It suffers all things that are imposed by its beloved, or that can happen for his sake, or that intervene in his service, cheerfully, sweetly, willingly; expecting that God should turn them into good, and instruments of felicity. 'Charity hopeth all things, endureth all things'.[5] Love is patient and content with anything, so it be together with its beloved.
5. Love is also impatient of anything that may displease the beloved person, hating all sin as the enemy of its friend; for love contracts all the same relations, and marries the same friendships and the same hatreds; and all affection to a sin is perfectly inconsistent with the love of God. Love is not divided between God and God's enemy: we must love God with all our heart; that is, give Him a

whole and undivided affection, having love for nothing else but such things which He allows, and which He commands or loves Himself.

6. Love endeavours for ever to be present, to converse with, to enjoy, to be united with its object; loves to be talking of him, reciting his praises, telling his stories, repeating his words, imitating his gestures, transcribing his copy in everything; and every degree of union and every degree of likeness is a degree of love; and it can endure anything but the displeasure and the absence of its beloved. For we are not to use God and religion as men use perfumes, with which they are delighted when they have them, but can very well be without them. True charity is restless, till it enjoys God in such instances in which it wants Him: it is like hunger and thirst, it must be fed, or it cannot be answered: and nothing can supply the presence, or make recompense for the absence of God, or of the effects of His favour and the light of His countenance.

7. True love in all accidents looks upon the beloved person, and observes his countenance, and how he approves or disapproves, looks sad or cheerful. He that loves God is not displeased at those accidents which God chooses; nor murmurs at those changes which He makes in His family; nor envies at those gifts He bestows; but chooses as He likes, and is ruled by His judgment, and is perfectly of His persuasion; loving to learn where God is the teacher, and being content to be ignorant or silent where He is not pleased to open Himself.

8. Love is careful of little things, of circumstances and measures, and little accidents; not allowing to itself any infirmity which it strives not to master, aiming at what it cannot yet reach, desiring to be of an angelical purity and of a perfect innocence, and fear every image of offence; is as much afflicted at an idle word as some at an act of adultery, and will not allow to itself so much anger as will disturb a child. And this is the curiosity and niceness of divine love: this is the fear of God, and is the daughter and production of love.

The measures and rules of Divine Love
But because this passion is pure as the brightest and smoothest

mirror, and, therefore, is apt to be sullied with every impurer breath, we must be careful that our love to God be governed by these measures.

1. That our love to God be sweet, even, and full of tranquillity; having in it no violence or transportations, but going on in a course of holy actions and duties, which are proportionable to our condition and present state. A new beginner in religion hath passionate and violent desires; but they must not be the measure of his actions: but he must consider his strength, his late sickness and the temptations of his condition, and stand at first upon his defence; not go to storm a strong fort, or attack a potent enemy, or do heroical actions fitter for giants in religion. Indiscreet violences and untimely forwardness are the rocks against which tender spirits often suffer shipwreck.

2. Let our love be prudent and without illusion; that is, that it express itself by proportion to His rules and measures. Love turns into doating, when religion turns into superstition: no degree of love can be imprudent, but the expressions may: we cannot love God too much, but we may proclaim it in undecent manners.

3. Let our love be firm, constant, and inseparable; not coming and returning like the tide, but descending like a never-failing river, ever running into the ocean of divine excellency, passing on in the channels of duty and a constant obedience, and never ceasing to be what it is, till it comes to be what it desires to be; even the immensity of a blessed eternity.

God is invisible, yet we feel Him in His blessings, He dwells in our hearts by faith, we feed on Him in the sacrament, and are made all one with Him in the incarnation of Jesus; yet, that we may the better enkindle and increase our love to God, the following advices are not useless:

Helps to increase our love to God
1. Every degree of inordinate affection to the things of this world, and every act of love to a sin, is a perfect enemy to the love of God.

2. Lay fetters and restraints upon the imaginative and fantastic part; because our fancy, being an imperfect and higher faculty, is usually pleased with the entertainment of shadows. Persons of fancy

have always the most violent loves. To this purpose it is good that we transplant the instruments of fancy into religion: and for this reason music was brought into churches, and ornaments, and perfumes, and comely garments, and solemnities, and decent ceremonies, that the busy and less discerning fancy, being bribed with its proper objects may be instrumental to a more celestial and spiritual love.

3. Remove solicitude or worldly cares, and multitudes of secular businesses; for if these take up our thoughts and our employments, they will also possess our passions; which, if they be filled with one object, cannot attend another, though more excellent.

4. Do not only choose the things of God, but secure your inclinations for God and for religion. For it will be a hard thing for a man to do such a personal violence to his first desires, and nothing can secure our loves to God but making religion to grow near the first desires of the soul.

5. Converse with God by frequent prayer. In particular, desire that your desires may be right, and love to have your affections regular and holy. Discover to Him all your wants; complain to Him of all your affronts; lay your misfortunes and your ill news before Him, call to Him for health, run to Him for counsel, beg of Him for pardon; and it is as natural to love Him to whom we make such addresses, and of whom we have such dependences, as it is for children to love their parents.

6. Consider the immensity of the divine love to us, expressed in all His providence: first, in His creation; secondly, in His conservation of us. For it is not my prince, or my patron, or my friend, that supports me or relieves my needs; but God, who made the corn that my friend sends me and who created the grapes. God, indeed, made him the instrument of His providence to me, as He hath made his own land or his own cattle to him. Thirdly, in giving His Son; fourthly in forgiving our sins; fifthly in adopting us to glory, — and it is not possible but for so great love we should give love again.

In the use of these instruments, love will grow in several knots and steps, like the sugar cane in India, according to a thousand varieties in the persons loving; and it will be great or less, in several persons, and in the same, according to his growth in Christianity. There are but two states of love; and those are labour of love, and the zeal of love: the first is duty; the second is perfection.

The two states of love to God

The least love must be obedient, pure, simple, and communicative; and must be expressive, according to our power, in the instances of duty, and must be love for love's sake; and for this love, martyrdom is the highest instance; that is, a readiness of mind rather to suffer any evil than to do any. Our blessed Saviour affirmed that no man had greater love than this; the highest point of duty, the greatest love, that God requires of man. And in this sense, he that loves God truly (though but with a beginning and tender love), yet he loves God with all his heart, which is the highest point of our duty and of God's charge upon us; and may yet increase with the increase of God: just as there are degrees of love to God among the saints, and yet each of them love Him with all their powers and capacities.

2. But the greater state of love is the zeal of love, which runs out into excrescences and suckers, like a fruitful and pleasant tree; producing fruits, not of a monstrous, but of an extraordinary and heroical greatness. Concerning which these cautions are to be observed.

Cautions and rules concerning zeal

1. If zeal be in the beginnings of our spiritual birth, or be short, sudden and transient, or be a consequent of a man's natural temper; or come upon any cause but after a long growth of a temperate and well-regulated love, it is to be suspected for passion and frowardness rather than the vertical point of love.[6]

2. That zeal only is good which hath temperate expressions. For let the affection boil as high as it can, yet if it boil over into irregular and strange actions, it will have but few, but will need many, excuses. Elijah was zealous and yet was so transported that he could not receive answer from God till by music he was recomposed.

3. Zeal must spend its greatest heat principally in those things that concern ourselves; but with great care and restraint in those that concern others.

4. Remember that zeal, being an excrescence of divine love, must in no sense contradict any action of love. Love to God includes love to our neighbour; and therefore no pretence of zeal for God's glory must make us uncharitable to our brother; for that is just so pleasing to God as hatred is an act of love.

5. That zeal that concerns others can spend itself in nothing but arts, and actions, and charitable instruments, for their good, and when it concerns the good of many that one should suffer, it must be done by persons of a competent authority, and in great necessity, in seldom instances according to the law of God or man; but never by private right, or for trifling accidents, or in mistaken propositions.

6. Zeal, in our own duty and personal deportment, is more safe than in matters of counsel tending towards perfection. Though in these instances there is not a direct sin, yet there is much trouble and some danger; as, if it be spent in the too-forward vows of chastity, and restraints of natural and innocent liberties.

7. Zeal may be let loose in personal, and spiritual actions, of direct duty; as in prayers, and acts of adoration: provided that no indirect act pass upon them to defile them; such as complacency and opinions of sanctity, censuring others, scruples and opinions of necessity, unnecessary fears, superstitious numberings of times and hours: but let the zeal be as forward, as devout, as it will, in the direct address and intercourse with God there is no danger, no transgression. Do all the parts of your duty as earnestly as if the salvation of all the world, and the whole glory of God, and all that you hope or desire, did depend upon every one action.

8. Let zeal be seated in the will and choice, and regulated with prudence and a sober understanding, not in the fancies and affections;[7] for these will make it full of noise and empty of profit; but that will make it deep and smooth, material and devout.

The sum is this: that zeal is not a direct duty, commanded for itself, but a forwardness of another duty, and is only acceptable when it advances the love of God and our neighbours, whose circumstances it is.[8] That zeal is only safe, only acceptable, which increases charity directly. St. Paul's zeal was expressed in preaching without any offerings or stipend, in travelling, in spending and being spent for his

flock, in suffering, in being willing to be accursed for love of the
people of God and his countrymen. Let our zeal be as great as his
was, so it be in affections to others, but not at all in angers against
them; in the first there is no danger, in the second there is no safety.
In brief, let your zeal (if it must be expressed in anger) be always
more severe against thyself than against others. [9]

(Note — The other part of love to God is love to our neighbour,
for which I have reserved the paragraph of alms.)

The external actions of religion

Religion teaches us to present to God our bodies as well as our souls,
for God is the Lord of both. Our bodies are to God a living sacrifice;
and to present them to God is holy and acceptable. [10]

The actions of the body as it serves to religion, and as it is distinguished from sobriety and justice, either relate to the word of God,
or to prayer, or to repentance, and make these kinds of external
actions of religion: first reading and hearing the word of God;
secondly fasting and corporal austerities, called by St. Paul bodily
exercise; thirdly, feasting, or keeping days of public joy and thanksgiving.

IV READING OR HEARING THE WORD OF GOD

Reading and hearing the word of God are instrumental especially to
faith, but consequently to all other graces of the spirit. It is all one to
us whether by the eye or by the ear the Spirit conveys his precepts to
us. If we hear St. Paul saying to us, that 'whoremongers and adulterers
God will judge' or read it in one of his epistles, we are equally and
sufficiently instructed. The Scriptures read are the same thing to us
which was preached by the disciples of our blessed Lord. There are
many that cannot read the word, and they must take it in by the ear;
and they that can read find the same word of God by the eye. The
word of God is all those commandments and revelations, those
promises and threatenings, the stories and sermons recorded in the
Bible; nothing else is the word of God that we know of by any

certain instrument. The good books and spiritual discourses, the sermons or homilies written or spoken by men, are explications and exhortations but of themselves they are not the word of God. In a sermon, the text only is in a proper sense to be called God's word : and yet good sermons are of great use and convenience for the advantages of religion. He that writes that sermon in a book, and publishes that book, hath preached to all that read it a louder sermon than could be spoken in a church. This I say that we may separate truth from error, popular opinions from substantial truths. For God preaches to us in the Scripture; good men preach to us when they, by popular arguments and human arts and compliances, expound and press any of those doctrines which God hath preached unto us in His holy word. But

First, the Holy Ghost is certainly the best preacher in the world, and the words of Scripture the best sermons.

Secondly, all the doctrine of salvation is plainly set down there, that the most unlearned person, by hearing it read, may understand all his duty. What can be plainer spoken than this, 'Thou shalt not kill'; 'Be not drunk with wine'; 'Husbands, love your wives'; 'Whatsoever ye would that men should do to you, do ye so to them?' The wit of man cannot more plainly tell us our duty, or more fully, than the Holy Ghost hath done already.

Thirdly, good sermons and good books are of excellent use; but yet they can serve no other end but that we practise the plain doctrines of Scripture.

Fourthly, that Abraham in the parable said concerning the brethren of the rich man, is here very proper: 'They have Moses and the prophets, let them hear them; but if they refuse to hear these, neither will they believe though one should arise from the dead to preach unto them'.[11]

Fifthly, reading the holy Scriptures is a duty expressly commanded us.[12]

But this duty is reduced to practice in the following rules.

Rules for hearing or reading the word of God
1. Set apart some portion of thy time, according to the opportunities

of thy calling and necessary employment, for the reading of Holy
Scripture; and if it be possible, every day read or hear some of it read.

2. When it is in your power to choose, accustom yourself to those
portions which are most plain and certain duty, and which contain
the story of the life and death of our blessed Saviour. Read the
gospels, the psalms of David; and especially those portions of
Scripture which by the wisdom of the Church, are appointed to be
publicly read upon Sundays and holidays, viz., the epistles and
gospels. In the choice of any other portions, you may advise with a
spiritual guide, that you may spend your time with most profit.

3. Fail not diligently to attend to the reading of Holy Scriptures
upon those days wherein it is most publicly and solemnly read in
churches; for at such times, besides the learning our duty, we obtain
a blessing along with it; it becoming to us, upon those days, a part of
the solemn divine worship.

4. When the word of God is read or preached to you, be sure you
be of a ready heart and mind, free from worldly cares and thoughts,
diligent to hear, careful to mark, studious to remember, and desirous
to practise and to live according to it: do not hear for any other end
but to become better in your life, and to be instructed in every good
work, and to increase in the love and service of God.

5. Beg of God that He would, by His Spirit, write the word in your
heart, and that you describe it in your life.

Concerning spiritual books and ordinary sermons [take in these advices also]

6. Let not a prejudice to any man's person hinder thee from receiving
good by his doctrine, if it be according to godliness; but (if occasion
offer it, or especially if duty present it to thee — that is, if it be
preached in that assembly where thou art bound to be present) accept
the word preached as a message from God, and the minister as His
angel in that ministration.

7. Consider and remark the doctrine in any discourse; and if the
preacher adds anything to comply with thy weakness, or to put thy
spirit into action or holy resolution, remember it, and make use of it.
Though thou beest a learned man, yet the same thing which thou
knowest already, if spoken by another, may be made active by that

application. The word of God does not work as a natural agent, but as a divine instrument: it does not prevail by the force of deduction and artificial discoursings only, but chiefly by way of blessing in the ordinance and in the ministry of an appointed person. At least obey the public order, and reverence the constitution, and give good example of humility, charity and obedience.

8. When Scriptures are read inquire with diligence and modesty into the meaning; but if homilies or sermons be made, consider whether all that be spoken be conformable to the Scriptures; for you must practise nothing but the command of God, nothing but the doctrine of Scriptures.

9. Use the advice of some spiritual or other prudent man for the choice of such books, as may be for the edification of thy spirit in the ways of holy living; esteem that time well accounted for, ever remembering that God, by hearing us in prayer, obliges us to hear Him, in His word, by what instrument soever it be conveyed.

A Prayer to be said before the hearing or reading the word of God
O eternal Jesus, let thy Holy Spirit be present with me in the reading or hearing Thy word, that I may do it humbly, reverently, without prejudice, with a mind ready and desirous to learn and to obey; that I may be readily furnished and instructed to every good work to the glory of Thy holy name. Amen.

V FASTING

Fasting without relation to spiritual ends, is a duty no where enjoined. But Christianity hath to do with it as it may be made an instrument of the Spirit, by subduing the lusts of the flesh, or removing any hindrances of religion. And it hath been practised by all ages of the church, and advised in order to three ministries: to prayer; to mortification of bodily lusts; and to repentance.

Rules for Christian fasting
1. Fasting, in order to prayer, ought to be a total fast from all things during the solemnity, unless a probable necessity intervene. Fasting

is commanded together with prayer — commanded (I say) by the church — to this end, that the spirit might be clearer and more angelical, when it is quitted in some proportions from the loads of flesh.

2. The help which fasting does to prayer cannot be served by changing flesh into fish, or milk meats into dry diet; but by turning much into little, or little into none at all, during the time of solemn and extraordinary prayer.

3. Fasting, as it is instrumental to prayer, must be attended with other aids, such as removing, for the time, all worldly cares and secular businesses. To which add alms; for upon the wings of fasting and alms holy prayer infallibly mounts to heaven.

4. When fasting is intended to serve the duty of repentance, it is then best chosen when it is short, sharp, and afflictive; that is, either a total abstinence from all nourishment; or to abstain from the bread of our desires, and only to take wholesome and less pleasing nourishment, vexing our appetite by the refusing a lawful satisfaction, since, in its petulancy and luxury, it preyed upon an unlawful.

5. Fasting designed for repentance must be ever joined with an extreme care that we fast from sin; for there is no greater folly or undecency in the world, than to commit that for which I am now judging and condemning myself.

6. He that fasts for repentance must, during that solemnity, abstain from all bodily delights, and the sensuality of all his senses and his appetites: for a man must not, when he mourns in his fast, be merry in his sport; weep at dinner, and laugh all day after; have a silence in his kitchen, and music in his chamber; judge the stomach, and feast the other senses. I deny not but a man may, in a single instance, punish a particular sin with a proper instrument, yet because the sorrow is of the whole man, no sense must rejoice, or be with any study or purpose feasted and entertained softly.

7. When fasting is intended to subdue a bodily lust, as the spirit of fornication, or the fondness of strong and impatient appetites, it must not be a sudden, sharp, and violent fast, but a state of fasting, a diet, a daily lessening our portion of meat and drink, and a choosing such a coarse diet, which may make the least preparation for the lusts of

the body. He that fasts three days without food will weaken other parts more than the ministers of fornication; and when the meals return as usually, they also will be served as soon as any. In the meantime, they will be supplied and made active by the accidental heat that comes with such violent fastings: for this is a kind of aerial devil; the prince that rules in the air is the devil of fornication; and he will be as tempting with the windiness of a violent fast as with the flesh of an ordinary meal. But a daily subtraction of the nourishment will introduce a less busy habit of body; and that will prove the more effectual remedy.

8. Fasting alone will not cure this devil, though it helps much towards it; what it is unable to do alone, in company with other instruments, and God's blessing upon them, it may effect.

9. All fasting must be done without any opinion of the necessity of the thing itself, without censuring others, with all humility; and just as a man takes physic, of which no man hath reason to be proud, and no man thinks it necessary but because he is in sickness, or in danger and disposition to it.

10. All fasts ordained by lawful authority are to be observed in order to the same purposes just as it is in private fasts; for there is no other difference, but that in public our superiors choose for us what in private we do for ourselves.

11. Fasts ordained by lawful authority are not to be neglected. It may be, one day of humiliation will not obtain the blessing, or alone kill the lust; yet it must not be despised if it can do anything towards it. An act of fasting is an act of self-denial; and, though it do not produce the habit, yet it is a good act.

12. When the principal end why a fast is prescribed is obtained by some other instrument, as if the spirit of fornication be cured by the rite of marriage, or by a gift of chastity; yet that person so eased is not freed from the fasts of the Church if those fasts can prudently serve any other end of religion, as that of prayer, or repentance, or mortification of some other appetite.

13. The fast publicly commanded, complying with public order, is reason enough to make obedience necessary, but this is an obligation of charity, not of justice.

14. All fasting is to be used with prudence and charity: for there is no end to which fasting serves but may be obtained by other instruments. This in our first care, that we secure our virtue; and next, that we secure our health, that we may the better exercise the labours of virtue; lest out of too much austerity, we bring ourselves to that condition that it be necessary to be indulgent to softness, ease and extreme tenderness.

15. Let not intemperance be the prologue or the epilogue to your fast, lest the fast be so far from taking off anything of the sin, that it be an occasion to increase it.

The benefits of fasting

Fasting is not to be commended as a duty, but as an instrument. It is called the nourishment of prayer, the restraint of lust, the wings of the souls, the diet of angels, the instrument of humility and self-denial; the purification of the spirit.

VI OF KEEPING FESTIVALS, AND DAYS HOLY TO THE LORD; PARTICULARLY THE LORD'S DAY

True natural religion, common to all nations and ages, did principally rely upon four great propositions; That there is one God; that God is nothing of those things which we see; that God takes care of all things below, and governs all the world; that He is the great Creator of all things, without Himself: and according to these were framed the four first precepts of the decalogue. We are eternally bound to confess God Almighty to be the maker of heaven and earth; but the manner of confessing it is changed from a rest, or a doing nothing to a speaking something; from a day to a symbol; we profess it in our creed, we confess it in our lives; we describe it by every line of our life, by every action of duty, by faith, and trust, and obedience. We keep one day in seven, and so confess the manner and circumstance of the creation; and we rest also, that we may tend holy duties. God's rest is to be understood to be a beholding and a rejoicing in His work finished: and therefore we truly represent God's rest, when we confess and rejoice in God's works and God's glory.

This the Christian Church does upon every day, but especially upon the Lord's day, which she hath set apart for this and all other offices of religion, determined by the resurrection of her dearest Lord, it being the first day of joy the Church ever had. And now, upon the Lord's day, we are not tied to the rest of the Sabbath, but to all the work of the Sabbath; and we are to abstain from bodily labour, not because it is a direct duty to us, as it was to the Jews; but because it is necessary, in order to our duty, that we attend to the offices of religion.

Rules for keeping the Lord's day and other Christian festivals

1. To distinguish festival days from common, do it not by lessening the devotion of ordinary days, but enlarge upon the holy day.

2. Upon the Lord's day, we must abstain from all works, except those which are matters of necessity, of common life, or of great charity; the labour of love and the labours of religion were not against the reason and the spirit of the commandment, for which the letter was decreed. Much more is it so on the Lord's day, where the letter is wholly turned into spirit, and there is no commandment of God but of spiritual and holy actions. Upon the Christian Sabbath necessity is to be served first; then charity; and then religion; for this is to give place to charity, in great instances, and in all cases God is to be worshipped in spirit and in truth.

3. The Lord's day, being the remembrance of a great blessing, must be a day of joy, festivity, spiritual rejoicing, and thanksgiving in remembering His mercies, in worshipping His excellences; in sending portions of pleasant meat to them for whom nothing is provided. And in all the arts and instruments of advancing God's glory, a memorial of the resurrection should be inserted, that the particular religion of the day be not swallowed up in the general. And of this we may the more easily serve ourselves, by rising seasonably in the morning to private devotion, and by retiring at the leisures and spaces of the day not employed in public offices.

4. Fail not to be present at the public hours and places of prayer, entering early and cheerfully, attending reverently and devoutly, abiding patiently during the whole office, piously assisting at the

prayers, and gladly also hearing the sermon; and at no hand omitting to receive the holy communion, when it is offered (unless some great reason excuse it), this being the great solemnity of thanksgiving, and a proper work of the day.

5. After the solemnities are past, visit sick persons, reconcile differences, do offices of neighbourhood, inquire into the needs of the poor, especially housekeepers, relieve them as they shall need, and as you are able; for then we truly rejoice in God, when we make our neighbours rejoice together with us.

6. Whatsoever you are to do yourself, as necessary, you are to take care that others also, who are under your charge, do in their station and manner. Provide on these days especially that they be instructed in the articles of faith and necessary parts of their duty.

7. Those who labour hard in the week must be eased upon the Lord's day; such ease being a great charity; but at no hand must they be permitted anything forbidden by the laws, anything that is scandalous, dangerous and apt to mingle sin with it; no games prompting to wantonness, to drunkenness, to quarrelling, to ridiculous and superstitious customs; but let their refreshments be innocent, and charitable, and of good report, and not exclusive of the duties of religion.

8. Neither God nor man hath passed any obligation upon us; we must preserve our Christian liberty, for even a good action may become a snare to us, if we make it an occasion of scruple by a pretence of necessity. He keeps the Lord's day best, that keeps it with most religion and with most charity.

9. What the church hath done in the article of the resurrection, she hath in some measure done of the nativity, of the ascension, and of the descent of the Holy Ghost at Pentecost — and so great blessings deserve an anniversary solemnity. And if, with great reason, the memory of the resurrection does return solemnly every week, it is but reason the other should return once a year. The commemoration of the articles of our Creed in solemn days and offices is a very excellent instrument to convey and imprint the sense and memory of it upon the spirits of the most ignorant persons. As a picture may with more fancy convey a story to a man than a plain narrative either

in word or writing, so a real representment, and an office of remembrance, and a day to declare it, is far more impressive than a picture.

10. The memories of the saints are precious to God, and therefore they ought also to be so to us; and such persons who serve God by holy living, industrious preaching, and religious dying, ought to have their names preserved in honour, and God be glorified in them, and their holy doctrines and lives published and imitated: and we, by so doing, give testimony to the article of the communion of saints. The holy day is best kept by giving God thanks for the excellent persons, apostles or martyrs, we them remember, and by imitating their lives; this all may do.

The mixed actions of Religion are — Prayer, Alms, Repentance, Receiving the Blessed Sacrament.

VII PRAYER

There is no greater argument in the world of our spiritual danger and unwillingness to religion, than the backwardness which most men have always, and all men have sometimes, to say their prayers; so weary of their length, so glad when they are done, so witty to excuse and frustrate an opportunity: and yet all is nothing but a desiring of God to give us the greatest and the best things we can need, and which can make us happy. It is a work so easy, so honourable, and to so great purpose, God hath not given us a greater argument of His willingness to have us saved, than by rewarding so easy a duty with so great blessings.

Motives to prayer
It is a duty commanded by God and His holy Son;
    It is an act of grace that we are admitted to run to Him as to a father, to lay open our wants, to complain of our burdens, to explicate our scruples, to beg remedy and ease, support and counsel, health and safety, deliverance and salvation; and
        God hath invited us to it by many gracious promises of hearing us;
        He hath appointed His Son to be the precedent of prayer.

Christ hath put it into the hands of men to rescind, or alter, all the decrees of God, by the power of prayers, and the prayers of men have saved cities and kingdoms from ruin; prayer hath raised dead men to life, hath stopped the violence of fire, shut the mouths of wild beasts, hath altered the course of nature, caused rain in Egypt, and drought in the sea. It cures diseases without physic, and makes physic to do the work of nature, and nature to do the work of grace, and grace to do the work of God; and it does miracles of accident and event. Yet prayer, that does all this, is, of itself, nothing but an ascent of the mind to God, a desiring things fit to be desired, and an expression of this desire to God as we can, and as becomes us. And our unwillingness to pray is nothing else but a not desiring what we ought passionately to long for; or if we do desire it, it is a choosing rather to miss our satisfaction and felicity than to ask for it.

There is no more to be said in this affair, but that we reduce it to practice, according to the following rules:

Rules for the practice of prayer

1. We must be careful that we never ask anything of God that is sinful, or that directly ministers to sin: for that is to ask God to dishonour Himself, and to undo us. We had need consider what we pray; for before it returns in blessing it must be joined with Christ's intercession, and presented to God. Let us principally ask of God power and assistances to do our duty, to glorify God, to do good works, to live a good life, to die in the fear and favour of God. These things God delights to give, and commands that we shall ask, and we may with confidence expect to be answered graciously.

2. We may lawfully pray to God for the gifts of the Spirit that minister to holy ends, such as are the gift of preaching, the spirit of prayer, good expression, a ready and unloosed tongue, good understanding, learning, opportunities to publish them, etc., with these only restraints: we may not ask them to serve our own ends, but only for God's glory, and then we shall have them, or a blessing for desiring them; we must submit to God's will, desiring Him to choose our employment, and to furnish our persons as He shall see expedient.

3. Whatsoever we may lawfully desire of temporal things, we may lawfully ask of God in prayer, and we may expect them, as they are promised. First, whatsoever is necessary to our life and being is promised to us; food to keep us alive, clothing to keep us from nakedness and shame: so long as our life is permitted to us, so long all things necessary to our life shall be ministered. We may be secure of maintenance, but not secure of our life: for that is promised, not this. We are not to make accounts by the measure of our desires, but by the measure of our needs. Secondly, whatsoever is convenient for us, pleasant, and modestly delectable, we may pray for; so we do it — (1) With submission to God's will; (2) Without impatient desires; (3) That it be not a trifle and inconsiderable, but a matter so grave and concerning as to be a fit matter to be treated on between God and our souls; (4) That we ask it not to spend upon our lusts, but for ends of justice, or charity, or religion, and that they be employed with sobriety.

4. He that would pray with effect must live with care and piety.[13] For although God gives to sinners the common blessings of life and chance, yet all sin is an impediment to prayer. Uncharitableness and wrath, hypocrisy in the present action, pride and lust, by defiling the body or the spirit, or by contracting some necessary ingredient in prayer (such as are mercy, humility, purity, and sincerity), do defile the prayer, and make it a direct sin in the circumstances or formality of the action.

5. All prayer must be made with faith and hope; that is, we must certainly believe[14] we shall receive the grace which God hath commanded us to ask; and that we ask things necessary, or at least good and innocent and profitable, and that our persons be gracious in the eyes of God: or else, what God hath promised to our natural needs He may, in many degrees, deny to our personal incapacity. We can but hope, after we have secured our good intentions. We are sure of a blessing, but in what instance we are not yet assured.

6. Our prayers must be fervent, intense, earnest, and importunate, when we pray for things of high concernment and necessity. 'Continuing instant in prayer'; 'striving in prayer'; 'labouring fervently in prayer'; 'night and day, praying exceedingly'; 'praying

always with all prayer': so St. Paul calls it.[15] 'Watching unto
prayer': so St. Peter.[16]. 'Praying earnestly': so St. James.[17] According
as our desires are, so are our prayers; and as our prayers are, so shall
be the grace, and so shall be the measure of glory. But this admits of
degrees according to the perfection or imperfection of our state of
life; but it hath no other measures, but ought to be as great as it can;
the bigger the better. In other things, we are to use a bridle: and as
we must limit our desires with submission to God's will, so also we
must limit the importunity of our prayers by the moderation and
term of our desires. Pray for it as earnestly as you may desire it.

7. Our desires must be lasting, and our prayers frequent, exercising
our hope, and faith, and patience, and long-suffering. This circumstance of duty our blessed Saviour taught, saying, that 'men ought
always to pray and not to faint'.[18] St. Paul calls it 'praying without
ceasing';[19] never giving over till we die.

8. Let the words of our prayers be pertinent, grave, material, not
studiously many, according to our need, sufficient to express our
wants. God hears us not the sooner for our many words, but much
the sooner for an earnest desire. In public, our devotion is to be
measured by the appointed office, and we are to support our spirit
with spiritual arts, that our private spirit may be a part of the public
spirit, and be adopted into the society and blessings of the communion of saints.

9. This is St. Paul's advice: 'Be careful for nothing; but in everything, by prayer and supplication with thanksgiving, let your requests
be made known unto God'.[20]

10. Whatever we beg of God, let us also work for it, if the thing be
matter of duty, for God loves to bless labour and to reward it, but not
to support idleness. Read Scriptures, and then pray to God for understanding. Pray against temptation; but you must also resist the devil,
and then he will flee from you. Ask of God competency of living; but
you must also work with your hands the things that are honest, that
ye may have to supply in time of need. We can but do our endeavour,
and pray for blessing, and then leave the success with God; and
beyond this we cannot deliberate, we cannot take care — but, so far,
we must.

1 1. To this purpose let every man study his prayers, for the body of our prayers is the sum of our duty; and as we must ask of God whatsoever we need, so we must labour for all that we ask. God's grace is necessary, and without it we can do nothing, and if we shall turn our prayers into precepts, we shall the easier turn our hearty desires into effective practices.

1 2. In all our prayers we must be careful to attend our present work, having a present mind, not wandering upon impertinent things, not distant from our words, much less contrary to them: and if our thoughts do wander, bring them back again with prudent and severe arts; by all means striving to obtain a diligent, a sober, an untroubled and a composed spirit.

1 3. Let your posture and gesture of body in prayers be reverent, grave, and humble: according to public order, for we may pray in bed, on horseback, 'everywhere'[21] and at all times, and in all circumstances; and some servants have not opportunity to pray so often as they would, unless they supply the appetites of religion by such accidental devotions.

1 4. 'Let prayers and supplications and giving of thanks be made for all men; for kings, and all that are in authority; for this is good and acceptable in the sight of God our Saviour'.[22] We, who must love our neighbours as ourselves, must also pray for them, and pray for secular prosperity to kings with more importunity than for ourselves; because they need more to enable their duty and government, and for the interests of religion and justice. This part of prayer is by the apostle called 'intercession'; in which, with special care, we are to remember our relatives, our family, our charge, our benefactors, our creditors; not forgetting to beg pardon and charity for our enemies, and protection against them.

1 5. Rely not on a single prayer in matters of great concernment; but make it as public as you can, by obtaining of others to pray for you; this being the great blessing of the communion of saints, that a prayer united is strong, like a well-ordered army; and God loves to be tied fast with such cords of love, and constrained by a holy violence.

1 6. Every time that is not seized upon by some other duty is

seasonable enough for prayer; but let it be performed as a solemn duty morning and evening, that God may begin and end all our business, that 'the outgoing of the morning and evening may praise him'; for so we bless God, and God blesses us.

Cautions for making vows

17. A vow to God is an act of prayer. It is not ill advice that we make vows to God in those cases in which we have great need or great danger. But let it be done according to these rules and cautions.

(1) That the matter of the vow be lawful. (2) That it be useful in order to religion or charity. (3) That it be grave, not trifling or impertinent; but great in our proportion of duty towards the blessing. (4) That it be of something to which formerly we were not obliged, or which we might have omitted without sin. (5) That it be done with prudence, lest we beg a blessing and fall into a snare. (6) Let every great prayer, and great need, and great danger, draw us nearer to God by the approach of a pious purpose to live more strictly; and let every mercy of God, answering that prayer, produce a real performance of it. (7) Let not young beginners in religion enlarge their hearts and straiten their liberty by vows of long continuance; nor, indeed, anyone else, without a great experience of himself and of all accidental dangers. Vows of single actions are safest, and proportionable to those single blessings ever begged in cases of sudden and transient importunities. (8) Let no action which is matter of question and dispute in religion ever become the matter of a vow. He vows foolishly that promises to God to live and die in such an opinion, in an article not necessary nor certain; or that, upon confidence of his present guide, binds himself for ever to the profession of what he may afterwards more reasonably contradict.

If we observe the former rules we shall pray piously and effectually; but even this duty hath in it some special temptations. The dangers are — Wandering thoughts; Tediousness of spirit.

Remedies against wandering thoughts in prayer

If we feel our spirits apt to wander in our prayers, and to retire into the world, or to things unprofitable;

1. Use prayer to be assisted in prayer; pray for the spirit of supplication, for a sober, fixed, and recollected spirit; and when to this you add a moral industry to be steady in your thoughts, whatsoever wanderings after this do return irremediably are a misery of nature and an imperfection, but no sin, while it is not cherished and indulged in.

2. In private it is not amiss to attempt the cure by reducing your prayers into collects and short forms of prayer, making voluntary interruptions, and beginning again, that the want of spirit and breath may be supplied by the short stages and periods.

3. When you have observed any considerable wandering of your thoughts, bind yourself to repeat that prayer again with actual attention, or else revolve the full sense of it in your spirit; and, possibly, the tempter may be driven away with his own art, and may cease to interpose his trifles when he perceives they do but vex the person into carefulness and piety.

4. Be sure, with actual attention, to say a hearty Amen to the whole prayer with one united desire, for that desire does the great work of the prayer, and secures the blessing, if the wandering thoughts were against our will, and disclaimed by contending against them.

5. Avoid multiplicity of businesses of the world; and labour for an evenness and tranquillity of spirit, smooth in all tempests of fortune; for so we shall better tend religion, when we are not torn in pieces with the cares of the world, and seized upon with low affections, passions, and interest.

6. It helps much if we say our prayers silently, without the voice, only by the spirit. For, in mental prayer if our thoughts wander we only stand still; when our mind returns we go on again: there is none of the prayer lost, as it is if our mouths speak and our hearts wander.

7. Remember that it is a great indecency to desire of God to hear those prayers a great part whereof we do not hear ourselves. If they be not worthy of our attention, they are far more unworthy of God's.

Signs of tediousness of spirit in our prayers and all actions of religion
Like the Jews, who complained that they were weary of the new moons, and their souls loathed the frequent return of their Sabbaths:

so do very many Christians, who (1) pray without fervour and earnestness of spirit; and (2) meditate but seldom, and that without fruit, or sense, or affection; or (3) who seldom examine their consciences, and when they do it, they do it but sleepily, slightly, without compunction, or hearty purpose, or fruits of amendment. (4) They enlarge themselves in the thoughts and fruition of temporal things, running for comfort to them only in any sadness and misfortune. (5) They love not to frequent the sacraments, nor any of the instruments of religion but love ease and a loose undisciplined life. (6) They obey not their superiors, but follow their own judgment when their judgment follows their affections, and their affections follow sense and worldly pleasures. (7) They neglect or do not attend to the inclinations to virtue which the Spirit of God puts into their soul. (8) They repent them of their vows and holy purposes, not because they discover any indiscretion in them, or intolerable inconvenience, but because they have within them labour; as the case now stands to them, displeasure. (9) They content themselves with the first degrees and necessary parts of virtue, and when they are arrived thither, they sit down as if they were come to the mountain of the Lord, and care not to proceed on toward perfection. (10) They enquire into all cases in which it may be lawful to omit a duty; and, though they will not do less than they are bound to do, yet they will do no more than needs must; for they do out of fear and self-love, not out of the love of God, or the spirit of holiness and zeal. He that will do no more than needs must, will soon be brought to omit something of his duty, and will be apt to believe less to be necessary than is.

Remedies against tediousness of spirit

1. Order your private devotions so that they become not arguments and causes of tediousness by their indiscreet length, but reduce your words, still keeping all the matter, and what is cut off in the length of your prayers supply in the earnestness of your spirit. The forms are made not less perfect, and the spirit is more, and the scruple is removed.

2. If we provide variety of forms of prayer, the change by consult-

ing with the appetites of fancy, may better entertain the spirit; we may be pleased to recite a hymn, when a collect seems flat to us and unpleasant; to sing rather than to say, or to sing this rather than that: we are certain that variety is delightful; and whether that be natural to us, or an imperfection, yet if it be complied with, it may remove some part of the temptation.

3. Break your office and devotion into fragments, for so no length can oppress your sickness of spirit; and, by often praying in such manner and in all circumstances, we shall habituate our souls to prayer: it will make everything relish of religion, and by degrees turn all into its nature.

4. Learn to abstract your thoughts and desires from pleasures and things of the world. Order your affairs so that religion may be propounded to you as a reward, and prayer as your defence, and holy actions as your security, and charity and good works as your treasure. Consider that all things else are satisfactions but to the brutish part of a man; and that these are the refreshments and relishes of that noble part of us by which we are better than beasts.

5. Do not seek for deliciousness and sensible consolations in the actions of religion, but only regard the duty and the conscience of it. In the beginning of religion most frequently, and at some other times, God complies with our infirmity, and encourages our duty with little overflowings of spiritual joy, and sensible pleasure, and delicacies in prayer, so as we seem to feel some little beam of heaven and great refreshments from the Spirit of consolation; yet this is not always safe for us to have, neither safe for us to expect and look for; it is a running after Him, not for the miracles but for the loaves; not for the wonderful things of God, and the desires of pleasing Him, but for the pleasures of pleasing ourselves. And as we must not judge our devotion to be barren or unfruitful when we want the overflowings of joy running over, so neither must we cease for want of them. If our spirits can serve God choosingly and greedily, out of pure conscience of our duty, it is better in itself, and more safe to us.

6. Whatsoever creates fear, or makes the spirit to dwell in a religious sadness, is apt to entender the spirit and make it devout and pliant to any part of duty; for a great fear, when it is ill-managed, is

the parent of superstition; but a discreet and well-guided fear produces religion.

7. Pray often, and you shall pray oftener. This rule relies not only upon reason derived from the nature of habits, which turn into a second nature, and make their actions easy, frequent, and delightful; but it relies upon a reason depending upon the nature and constitution of grace, and increases itself, naturally growing from grains to huge trees, from moments to eternity. But be sure not to omit your usual prayers without great reason, though without sin it may be done; because after you have omitted something, in a little while you will be past the scruple of that, and begin to be tempted to leave out more. Keep yourself up to your usual forms; you may enlarge when you will; but do not contract or lessen them without a very probable reason.

8. Let a man frequently and seriously, by imagination, place himself upon his death-bed, and consider what great joys he shall have for the remembrance of every day well spent, and what then he would give that he had so spent all his days. He resigns his soul with peace into the hands of God, who hath lived in the peace of God and the works of religion in his lifetime. This consideration is of a real event; it is of a thing that will certainly come to pass.

9. To this may be useful that we consider the easiness of Christ's yoke, the excellences and sweetnesses that are in religion, the peace of conscience, the joy of the Holy Ghost, the rejoicing in God, the simplicity and pleasure of virtue, the intricacy, trouble and business of sin. If we are weary of the labours of religion, we must eternally sit still and do nothing; for whatsoever we do contrary to it is infinitely more full of labour, care, difficulty and vexation.

10. Tediousness of spirit is the beginning of the most dangerous condition and estate in the whole world. For it is a great disposition to the sin against the Holy Ghost: it is apt to bring a man to backsliding and the state of unregeneration; to make him return to his vomit and his sink; and either to make the man impatient, or unsatisfied, irksome, and desperate. It is better that he had never known the way of godliness than, after the knowledge of it, that he should fall away. There is not in the world a greater sign that the spirit of

reprobation is beginning upon a man, than when he is habitually and constantly, or very frequently, weary, and slights or loathes holy offices.

11. The last remedy that preserves the hope of such a man to the state of zeal and the love of God, is a pungent, sad, and a heavy affliction; not desperate, but recreated with some intervals of kindness, or hopes of deliverance; which condition if a man shall fall into, by the grace of God he is likely to recover; but if this help him not, it is infinite odds but he will quench the Spirit.

A Form of Prayer or intercession for all estates of people in the Christian Church: and proper to be said in our preparation to the Holy Sacrament, or on the day of celebration.

1. For ourselves

O Thou gracious Father of mercy, have mercy upon Thy servants, who bow our heads, knees, and hearts to Thee: pardon and forgive us all our sins; give us the grace of repentance, and a strict obedience to Thy word: strengthen us in the inner man with the power of Thy Holy Ghost for all the parts and duties of our calling and holy living; preserve us for ever in the unity of the holy catholic church, and in the integrity of the Christian faith, and in the love of God and of our neighbours, and in hope of life eternal. Amen.

2. For the whole Catholic Church

O holy Jesus, preserve whom Thou hast purchased and redeemed and cleansed with Thy blood; the whole Catholic Church from one end of the earth to the other. Preserve her safe from schism, heresy, and sacrilege. Unite all her members with the bands of faith, hope, and charity, and an external communion, when it shall seem good in Thine eyes. Let the daily sacrifice of prayer and sacramental thanksgiving never cease, but forever prevail for the obtaining for every of its members grace and blessing pardon and salvation. Amen.

3. For all Christian Kings, Princes, and Governors

O King of kings, and Prince of all the rulers of the earth, give Thy grace and Spirit to all Christian princes, the spirit of wisdom and counsel, the spirit of government and godly fear. Grant unto them to live in peace and honour, that their people may love and fear them, and they may love and fear God. Speak good unto their hearts concerning the Church, that they may be nursing fathers to it, compassionate to the wants of the poor, and the groans of the oppressed; that they may not vex or kill the Lord's people

with unjust or ambitious wars, but may feed the flock of God, and may enquire after
and do all things which may promote peace, public honesty, and holy religion; so
administering things present that they may not fail of the everlasting glories of the
world to come, where all Thy faithful people shall reign kings for ever. Amen.

4. For all the orders of them that minister about holy things

O Thou great Shepherd and Bishop of our souls, give unto Thy servants the
ministers of the mysteries of Christian religion, the spirit of prudence and sanctity,
faith and charity, confidence and zeal, diligence and watchfulness, that they may
declare Thy will faithfully, dispense Thy sacraments rightly, and intercede with Thee
graciously and acceptably for Thy servants. Grant, O Lord, that by a holy life and a
true belief, by well doing and patient suffering they may glorify Thee, and, after a
plentiful conversion of sinners from the errors of their ways, they may shine like the
stars in glory. Amen.

Give unto Thy servants the bishops, a discerning spirit, that they may lay hands
suddenly on no man, but may depute such persons to the ministries of religion who
may adorn the gospel of God, and whose lips may preserve knowledge, and such who
by their good preaching and holy living may advance the service of the Lord Jesus.
Amen.

5. For our nearest relatives, as husband, wife, children, family, etc.

O God of infinite mercy, let Thy loving mercy and compassion descend upon the head
of Thy servants (my wife or husband, children, and family) : be pleased to give them
health of body and of spirit, a competent portion of temporals, so as may with comfort
support them in their journey to heaven : preserve them from all evil and sad accidents,
defend them in all assaults of their enemies, sanctify their hearts and words and purposes; that we all may, by the bands of obedience and charity, be united to our Lord
Jesus. Amen.

6. For our parents, our kindred in the flesh, our friends and
benefactors

O God, merciful and gracious, who hast made (my parents) my friends, and my
benefactors, ministers of Thy mercy, depute Thy holy angels to guard their persons,
Thy Holy Spirit to guide their souls, Thy providence to minister to their necessities;
and let Thy grace and mercy preserve them, through Jesus Christ. Amen.

7. For all that lie under the rod of war, famine, pestilence

O Lord God Almighty, Thou art our Father, we are Thy children. Let health and peace
be within our dwellings; let righteousness and holiness dwell for ever in our hearts,
and be expressed in all our actions.

O merciful God, say unto the destroying angel, 'It is enough'; let Thy hand cover Thy servants and hide us from the present anger; that though we walk through the valley of the shadow of death, we may fear no evil, and suffer none. Those smitten, support with Thy staff, and visit them with Thy mercies and salvation, through Jesus Christ. Amen.

8. For all women with child, and for unborn children

O Lord God, who art the Father of them that trust in Thee, and shewest mercy to a thousand generations of them that fear Thee; have mercy upon all women great with child; be pleased to give them a joyful and a safe deliverance: and let Thy grace preserve the fruit of their wombs, and conduct them to the holy sacrament of baptism; that they, by Thy Spirit, may live to the glory of God, to the comfort of their parents and friends, to the edification of the Christian commonwealth, and the salvation of their own souls, through Jesus Christ. Amen.

9. For all estates of men and women in the Christian Church

O holy God, King eternal, out of the infinite storehouses of Thy grace and mercy, give unto all virgins chastity and a religious spirit; to all persons dedicated to Thee and to religion, continence and meekness and active zeal and an unwearied spirit; to all married pairs, faith and holiness; to widows and fatherless, and all that are oppressed, Thy patronage, comfort, and defence; to all Christian women simplicity and modesty, humility and chastity, patience and charity; give unto the poor, to all that are robbed and spoiled of their goods, a competent support, and a contented spirit, and a treasure in heaven hereafter; give unto prisoners and captives, to them that toil in the mines, and row in the galleys, strength of body and of spirit, liberty and redemption, comfort and restitution; to all that travel by land, Thy angel for their guide, and a holy and prosperous return; to all that travel by sea, freedom from pirates and shipwreck, and bring them to the haven where they would be; to distressed and scrupulous consciences, to melancholy and disconsolate persons, to all that are afflicted with evil, and unclean spirits, give a light from heaven, great grace and proportionable comforts, and timely deliverance; give them patience and resignation; let their sorrows be changed into grace and comfort, and let the storm waft them certainly to the regions of rest and glory.

Lord God of mercy, give to Thy martyrs, confessors, and all Thy persecuted, constancy and prudence, boldness and hope, a full faith, and a never-failing charity. To all who are condemned to death, do Thou minister comfort, a strong, a quiet, and a resigned spirit; take from them the fear of death, and all remaining affections to sin, and all imperfections of duty, and cause them to die full of grace, full of hope. And give to all faithful, and particularly to those who have recommended themselves to the prayers of Thy unworthy servant, a supply of all their needs temporal and spiritual, and, according to their several states and necessities, rest and peace, pardon and refreshment; and show us all mercy in the day of judgment. Amen.

Give, O Lord, to the magistrates equity, sincerity, courage, and prudence, that they may protect the good, defend religion, and punish the wrong-doers. Give to the nobility wisdom, valour, and loyalty; to merchants, justice and faithfulness: to all artificers and labourers, truth and honesty; to our enemies, forgiveness and brotherly kindness.

Preserve to us the heavens and the air in healthful influence and disposition, the earth in plenty, the kingdom in peace and good government, our marriages in peace and sweetness and innocence of society, Thy people from famine and pestilence, our houses from burning and robbery, our persons from being burnt alive, from banishment and prison, from widowhood and destitution, from violence of pains and passions, from tempests and earthquakes, from inundation of waters, from rebellion or invasion, from impatience and inordinate cares, from tediousness of spirit and despair, from murder, and all violent, accursed, and unusual deaths, from the surprise of sudden and violent accidents, from passionate and unreasonable fears, from all Thy wrath, and from all our sins, good Lord, deliver and preserve Thy servants for ever. Amen.

Repress the violence of all implacable, warring, and tyrant nations; bring home unto Thy fold all that are gone astray; call into the Church all strangers; increase the number and holiness of Thine own people; bring infants to ripeness of age and reason; confirm all baptized people with Thy grace and with Thy Spirit; instruct the novices and new Christians; let a great grace and merciful providence bring youthful persons safely and holily through the indiscretions, and passions, and temptations of their younger years; and to those whom Thou hast or shalt permit to live to the age of a man, give competent strength and wisdom; take from them covetousness and churlishness, pride and impatience; fill them full of devotion and charity, repentance and sobriety, holy thoughts and longing desires after heaven and heavenly things; give them a holy and a blessed death, and to us all a joyful resurrection, through Jesus Christ our Lord. Amen.

VIII OF ALMS

Love is as communicative as fire, as busy and as active, and it hath four twin-daughters, extreme like each other; and but that the doctors of the school have done, as Thamar's midwife did, who bound a scarlet thread, something to distinguish them, it would be very hard to call them asunder. Their names are Mercy, Beneficence or well-doing; Liberality; and Alms; which, by a special privilege, hath obtained to be called after the mother's name, and is commonly called Charity. The first or eldest is seated in the affection: and it is that which all the others must attend; for mercy, without alms, is acceptable when the person is disabled to express outwardly what he heartily desires. But alms, without mercy, are like prayers without devotion, or religion without humility. Beneficence, or well-doing, is a promptness and nobleness of mind, making us to do offices of courtesy and humanity to all sorts of persons in their need, or out of their need. Liberality is a disposition of mind opposite to covetous-ness; and consists in the despite and neglect of money upon just occasions, and relates to our friends, children, kindred, servants, and other relatives. But alms is a relieving the poor and needy. The first and the last only are duties of Christianity. Liberality increases the degree of alms, making our gift greater; and beneficence extends it to more persons and orders of men, spreading it wider. The former makes us sometimes to give more than we are able; and the latter gives to more than need by the necessity of beggars; whereas, properly, alms are doles and largesses to the necessitous and calamitous people, giving remedies to their miseries.

Mercy and alms are to the body and soul of that charity which we must pay to our neighbour's need; that the great inequality in the possessions and accidents of men might be reduced to some temper and evenness; and the most miserable person might be reconciled to some sense and participation of felicity.

Works of mercy, or the several kinds of corporal alms
The works of mercy are so many as the affections of mercy have objects, or as the world hath kinds of misery. Men want meat, or drink, or clothes, or a house, or liberty, or attendance, or a grave. In proportion to these, seven works are usually assigned to mercy, and there are seven kinds of corporal alms reckoned:

To feed the hungry;[23]

To give drink to the thirsty;
Or clothes to the naked;
To redeem captives;
To visit the sick;
To entertain strangers;
To bury the dead.[24]
But many more may be added. Such as are —
To give physic to sick persons;
To bring cold and starved people to warmth and to the fire — for sometimes clothing will not do it, or this may be done when we cannot do the other;
To lead the blind in right ways;
To lend money;
To forgive debts;
To remit forfeitures;
To mend highways and bridges;
To guide wandering travellers;
To ease their labours by accommodating their work with apt instruments, or their journey with beasts of carriage;
To deliver the poor from their oppressors;
To die for my brother;
To pay maidens' dowries, and to procure for them honest and chaste marriages.

Works of spiritual alms and mercy are —
To teach the ignorant;
To counsel doubting persons;
To admonish sinners diligently, prudently, seasonably, and charitably: to which also may be reduced, provoking and encouraging to good works;[25]
To comfort the afflicted;
To pardon offenders;
To suffer and support the weak;[26]
To pray for all estates of men, and for relief to all their necessities.
To which may be added —
To punish or correct refractoriness;

To be gentle and charitable in censuring the actions of others;

To establish the scrupulous, wavering, and inconstant spirits;

To confirm the strong;

Not to give scandal;

To quit a man of his fear;

To redeem maidens from prostitution and publication of their bodies.

To both these kinds a third also may be added of a mixed nature, partly corporal and partly spiritual: such are — reconciling enemies; erecting public schools of learning; maintaining lectures of divinity; erecting colleges of religion and retirement from the noises and more frequent temptations of the world; finding employment for un-busied persons, and putting children to honest trades. For the particulars of mercy or alms cannot be narrower than men's needs are. The kinds are too many to be discoursed of particularly; only our blessed Saviour, in the precept of alms, uses the instances of relieving the poor, and forgiveness of injuries. But alms in general are to be disposed of according to the following rules:

Rules for giving alms

1. Let no man do alms of that which is none of his own. He that gives the poor what is not his own, makes himself a thief, and the poor the receivers.

2. Of money unjustly taken, and yet voluntarily parted with, we may and are bound to give alms; such as is money given and taken for false witness, bribes, simoniacal contracts; because the receiver hath no right to keep it, nor the giver any right to recall it; it is unjust money, and yet payable to none but the supreme Lord (who is the person injured), and to His delegates, that is, the poor.

3. There is some sort of gain that hath in it no injustice, properly so called; but it is unlawful and filthy lucre; such as hire taken for disfiguring one's self, the wages of such as make unjust bargains, and of harlots. The person must repent and leave the crime, and then minister to the poor.

4. He that gives alms must do it in mercy; that is, out of a true sense of the calamity of his brother. Against this rule they offend who

give alms out of custom, or to upbraid the poverty of the other, or to make him mercenary and obliged, or with any unhandsome circumstances.

5. He that gives alms must do it with a single eye and heart, that is, without designs to get the praise of men; for Christ intended only to provide against pride and hypocrisy when He bade alms to be given in secret; it being otherwise one of His commandments, 'that our light should shine before men': this is more excellent; that is more safe.

6. He who hath done a good turn should so forget it as not to speak of it; but he that boasts it, or upbraids it, hath paid himself and lost the nobleness of the charity.

7. Give alms with a cheerful heart and countenance; 'not grudgingly or of necessity, for God loveth a cheerful giver';[27] give quickly, when the power is in thy hand, and the need is in thy neighbour, and thy neighbour at the door. He gives twice that relieves speedily.

8. According to thy ability give to all men that need;[28] and in equal needs give first to good men rather than to bad men; and if the needs be unequal, do so too, provided that the need of the poorest be not violent or extreme; but no difference of virtue or vice can make the ease of one beggar equal with the life of another.

9. Give no alms to vicious persons if such alms will support their sin, as if they will continue in idleness. Such persons, when they are reduced to very great want, must be relieved in such proportions as may not relieve their dying lust, but may refresh their faint or dying bodies.

10. The best objects of charity are poor house-keepers that labour hard, and are burdened with many children; or gentlemen fallen into sad poverty, especially if by innocent misfortunes; persecuted persons; widows; and fatherless children, putting them to honest trades or schools of learning. And search into the needs of persons that have nothing left them but misery and modesty; enquire them out. Convey relief unto them so as we do not make them ashamed.

11. Give, looking for nothing again: give to children, to old men, to the unthankful, and the dying, and to those you shall never see

again; for else your alms or courtesy is not charity, but traffic and merchandise; and omit not to relieve the needs of your enemy; for so, possibly, you may win him to yourself; but do you intend the winning him to God.

12. Trust not your alms to under-dispensers: by which is not only intended the securing your alms in the right channel, but the humility of your person, which the apostle calls 'the labour of love'. And if you converse in hospitals and alms-houses, and minister with your own hand, what your heart hath first decreed, you will find your heart endeared and made familiar with the needs and with the persons of the poor, those excellent images of Christ.

13. 'He that hath two coats must give to him that hath none'; that is, he that hath beyond his need must give that which is beyond it. Only among needs, we are to reckon not only what will support our life, but also what will maintain the decency of our estate and person. But yet, if we do give more than we are able, we have St. Paul for our encouragement; we have Christ for our counsellor; we have God for our rewarder. It cannot be denied but, in the expenses of all liberal and great personages, many things might be spared; some unnecessary and imprudent feasts, some garments too costly, some unnecessary lawsuits, some vain journeys; and when we are tempted to such needless expenses, we shall find it with more profit to be laid out upon the poor members of Christ than upon our own with vanity. But I am not ignorant that great variety of clothes always have been permitted to princes and nobility and others in their proportion; and they usually give those clothes as rewards to servants, and other persons needful enough, and then they may serve their own fancy and their duty too; but it is but reason and religion to be careful that they be given to such only where duty, or prudent liberality, or alms, determine them; but in no sense let them do it so as to minister to vanity, to luxury, to prodigality. If we once give our minds to the study and arts of alms, we shall find ways enough to make this duty easy, profitable, and useful.

He that plays at any game must resolve beforehand to be indifferent to win or lose; but if he gives to the poor all that he wins, it is better than to keep it to himself; but it were better yet that he lay by so much as he is willing to lose, and let the game alone.

Keeping the fasting-days of the Church, we may, from wanting meals, find a considerable relief for the poor. But if we be not willing sometimes to fast, that our brother may eat, we should ill die for him. Christ gave Himself to shame and death to redeem His enemies.

Learn of the frugal man, and only avoid sordid actions, and turn good husband: and why should we not do as much for charity, as for covetousness; for heaven, as for the fading world?

14. In giving alms to beggars it is better to give little to each, that we may give to the more; but in charities of religion, as building hospitals, colleges, and houses for devotion, it is better to unite our alms than to disperse them; to make a noble relief than to support only natural needs.

15. The eye is the sense of mercy, and enkindles pity, and pity produces alms: the providence of God hath fitted our charity with circumstances. He that is in Thy sight or in Thy neighbourhood is fallen into the lot of Thy charity.

16. If thou hast no money[29] yet thou must have mercy, and art bound to pity the poor, and pray for them, and throw thy holy desires and devotions into the treasure of the Church; and if thou doest what thou art able, be it little or great, corporal or spiritual, the charity of alms or the charity of prayers, a cup of wine or a cup of water, if it be but love to the brethren,[30] or a desire to help all or any of Christ's poor, it shall be accepted according to that a man hath, not according to that he hath not.[31] For love is all this, and all the other commandments: and it will express itself where it can; and where it cannot, yet it is love still; and it is also sorrow that it cannot.

Motives to charity

1. There is no one duty which our blessed Saviour did recommend to His disciples with so repeated an injunction as this of charity and alms.[32] To which add the words spoken by our Lord, 'It is better to give than to receive'.

2. Charity and alms is that whereby Christ shall declare justice and mercy. Martyrdom itself is no otherwise involved, but as it is the greatest charity.

3. Christ made Himself the greatest and daily example of alms or charity. He went up and down doing good, preaching the gospel, and healing all diseases: and God the Father is imitable by us in nothing but in purity and mercy.

4. Alms given to the poor redound to the giver both temporal and eternal.[33]

5. Our forgiveness and mercy to others are the very rule and proportion of our confidence and hope, and our prayer to be forgiven ourselves.[34]

6. When a poor man begs for Christ's sake, if he have reason to ask, for Christ's sake give it him if thou canst.

7. It is one of the wings of prayer by which it flies to the throne of grace.

8. It crowns all the works of piety.

9. It causes thanksgiving to God on our behalf.

10. And the bowels of the poor bless us and they pray for us.

11. And that portion of our estate, out of which a tenth, or a fifth, or a twentieth, or some offering to God for religion and the poor goes forth, certainly returns with a great blessing upon all the rest. It is like the widow's barrel of meal, it consumed not as long as she fed the prophet.

12. The sum of all is contained in the words of our blessed Saviour: 'Give alms of such things as you have, and behold all things are clean unto you'.

13. Charity or mercy is the peculiar character of God's elect, and a sign of predestination, which advantage we are taught by St. Paul: 'Put on, therefore, as the elect of God, holy and beloved, bowels of mercy, kindness &c. forbearing one another, and forgiving one another, if any man have a quarrel against any'.[35] The result of all which we may read in the words of St. Chrysostom: 'To know the art of alms is greater than to be crowned with the diadem of kings; and yet to convert one soul is greater than to pour out ten thousand talents into the baskets of the poor'.

But because giving alms is an act of the virtue of mercifulness, our endeavour must be, by proper arts, to mortify the parents of unmercifulness, which are: (1) Envy; (2) Anger; (3) Covetousness: in which we may be helped by the following rules or instruments.

REMEDIES AGAINST UNMERCIFULNESS AND UNCHARITABLENESS

1 Against envy

Against envy I shall use the same argument I would use to persuade a man from the fever of the dropsy.

1. Because it is a disease; it is so far from having pleasure in it, or a temptation to it, that it is full of pain, a great instrument of vexation.

2. It is nothing but a direct resolution never to enter into heaven by the way of noble pleasure taken in the good of others.

3. It is most contrary to God,

4. And a just contrary state to the felicities and actions of heaven, where every star increases the light of the other, and the multitude of guests makes the eternal meal more festival.

5. It is perfectly the state of hell and the passion of devils; for they do nothing but despair in themselves, and envy others' quiet or safety and yet cannot rejoice either in their good or in their evil, although they endeavour to hinder that and procure this, with all the devices and arts of malice and of a great understanding.

6. Envy can serve no end in the world; it cannot please anything, nor do anything, nor hinder anything, but the content and felicity of him that hath.

7. Envy can never pretend to justice, as hatred and uncharitableness sometimes may; for there may be causes of hatred, and I may have wrong done me, and then hatred hath some pretence, though no just argument, but no man is unjust or injurious for being prosperous or wise.

8. And therefore many men profess to hate another, but no man owns envy. Envious men, being like wasps and caterpillars, that delight most to devour ripe and most excellent fruits.

9. It is of all crimes the basest; for malice and anger are appeased with benefits, but envy is exasperated, as envying to fortunate persons both their power and their will to do good, and never leaves murmuring till the envied person be levelled. For if his neighbour

be made miserable the envious man is apt to be troubled : like him
that is so long unbuilding the turrets, till all the roof is low or flat,
or that the stones fall upon the lower buildings and do a mischief,
that the man repents of.

2 *Against anger, by way of exercise*
The next enemy to mercifulness and the grace of alms is anger;
against which there are proper instruments both in prudence and
religion.

1. Prayer is the great remedy against anger; for it must suppose it
in some degree removed before we pray, and then it is the more
likely it will be finished when the prayer is done.

2. If anger arises in thy breast, instantly seal up thy lips, and let it
not go forth; for like fire, when it wants vent, it will suppress
itself. Angry passion is a fire, and angry words are like breath to fan
them; together they are like steel and flint sending out fire by mutual
collision. Some men will discourse themselves into passion; and if
their neighbour be enkindled too, together they flame with rage and
violence.

3. Humility is the most excellent natural cure for anger in the
world; for he that by daily considering his own infirmities and
failings, makes the error of his neighbour or servant to be his own
case, and remembers that he daily needs God's pardon and his
brother's charity, will not be apt to rage at the levities, or misfortunes, or indiscretions of another.

4. Consider the example of Jesus, who suffered all the con-
tradications of sinners, and received all affronts and reproaches of
malicious, rash, and foolish persons, and yet in all them, was as
dispassionate and gentle as the morning sun in autumn. For if
innocence itself did suffer so great injuries and disgraces, it is no
great matter for us quietly to receive all the calamities of fortune,
and indiscretion of servants, and mistakes of friends, and unkind-
nesses of kindred, and rudenesses of enemies, since we have
deserved these and worse, even hell itself.

5. If we be tempted to anger in the actions of government and
discipline to our inferiors (in which case anger is permitted so far

as it is prudently instrumental to government, and only is a sin when
it is excessive and unreasonable, and apt to disturb our own discourse, or to express itself in imprudent words or violent actions),
let us propound to ourselves the example of God the Father, who, at
the same time and with the same tranquillity, decreed heaven and
hell; and at the day of judgment, God shall not be at all inflamed
or shaken in His essential seat and centre of tranquillity and joy.
And if at first the cause seems reasonable, yet defer to execute thy
anger till thou mayest better judge. For, as Phocion told the
Athenians, who upon the first news of the death of Alexander were
ready to revolt, 'Stay a while; for if the king be not dead, your haste
will ruin you; but if he be dead, your stay cannot prejudice your
affairs, for he will be dead to-morrow as well as today': so if thy
servant or inferior deserves punishment, staying till tomorrow will
not make him innocent; but it may possibly preserve thee, so by
preventing thy striking a guiltless person, or being furious for a
trifle.

6. Remove from thyself all provocations and incentives to anger;
especially, (1) Games of chance and great wager. Patroclus killed his
friend, the son of Amphidamas, in his rage and sudden fury, rising
upon a cross game at tables. Such also are petty anxieties, of those
external things, and do not spend a passion upon them, for it is
more than they are worth. (2) In not heaping up, with an ambitious
or curious prodigality, any very curious or choice utensils, seals,
jewels, glasses, precious stones; because those very many accidents
which happen in the spoiling or loss of these rarities, are, in event,
an irresistible cause of violent anger. (3) Do not entertain nor
suffer talebearers; for they abuse our ears first, and then our
credulity, and then steal our patience, and, it may be for a lie; and
if it be true, the matter is not considerable; or if it be, yet it is
pardonable. And we may always escape by not hearing slanders; or
by not believing them; or by not regarding the thing; or by
forgiving the person. (4) Choose as much as we can to live with
peaceable persons, for that prevents the occasions of confusion;
and if we live with prudent persons, they will not easily occasion
our disturbance. But because these things are not in many men's

power, therefore I propound this rather as a felicity than a remedy or a duty, and an act of prevention than of cure.

7. Be not inquisitive into the affairs of other men, nor the faults of thy servants, nor the mistakes of thy friends; but what is offered to you, use according to the former rules; but do not thou go out to gather sticks to kindle a fire to burn thine own house. And add this: 'If my friend said or did well in that for which I am angry, I am in the fault, not he; but if he did amiss, he is in the misery, not I: for either he was deceived, or he was malicious; and either of them both is all one with a miserable person; and that is an object of pity, not of anger'.

8. Use all reasonable discourses to excuse the faults of others; considering that there are many circumstances of time, of person, of accident, of sorrow for doing it; and it is well that we take any good in exchange for the evil done or suffered.

9. Upon the arising of anger, instantly enter into a deep consideration of the joys of heaven, or the pains of hell; for 'fear and joy are naturally apt to appease this violence'.

10. In contentions be always upon the defensive, not the assaulting part; give a gentle answer, receiving the furies and indiscretions of the other, like a stone into a bed of moss and you shall find it sit down quietly; whereas anger and violence make the contention loud and long, and injurious to both the parties.

11. In the actions of religion, be careful to temper all thy instances with meekness; and if thou beest apt to be angry, neither fast violently, nor entertain the too forward heats of zeal, but secure thy duty with constant and regular actions, and a good temper of body, with convenient refreshments and recreations.

12. If anger rises suddenly and violently, first restrain it with consideration; and then let it end in a hearty prayer for him that did the real or seeming injury. The former of the two stops its growth, and the latter quite kills it, and makes amends for its monstrous and involuntary birth.

3 *Against anger, by way of consideration*

1. Anger is a professed enemy to counsel; it is a direct storm in

which no man can be heard to speak or call from without: for if you counsel gently, you are despised; if you urge it and be vehement, you provoke it more. Be careful, therefore, to lay up beforehand a great stock of reason and prudent consideration, that, like a besieged town, you may be provided for, and be defensible from within since you are not likely to be relieved from without. Anger is not to be suppressed but by something that is as inward as itself, and more habitual.

2. Of all passions it endeavours most to make reason useless.

3. That it is a universal poison of an infinite object; no man was ever so amorous as to love a toad, none so envious as to repine at the condition of the miserable, no man so timorous as to fear a dead bee; but anger is troubled at every thing, and every man, and every accident, and, therefore, unless it be suppressed it will make a man's condition restless.

4. If it proceeds from a great cause it turns to fury; if from a small cause it is peevishness; and so is always either terrible or ridiculous.

5. It makes a man's body monstrous, deformed, and contemptible; the voice horrid; the eyes cruel; the face pale or fiery; the gait fierce; the speech clamorous and loud.

6. It is neither manly nor ingenuous.

7. It proceeds from softness of spirit and pusillanimity; which makes that women are more angry than men, sick persons more than the healthful, old men more than young, unprosperous and calamitous people than the blessed and fortunate.

8. It is a passion fitter for flies and insects, than for persons professing nobleness and bounty.

9. It is troublesome not only to those that suffer it, but to them that behold it; there being no greater incivility of entertainment, than for the cook's fault, or the negligence of the servants, to be cruel, or outrageous, or unpleasant in the presence of the guests.

10. It makes marriage to be a necessary and unavoidable trouble; friendships, and societies, and familiarities to be intolerable.

11. It multiplies the evils of drunkenness, and makes the levities of wine to run into madness.

12. It makes innocent jesting to be the beginning of tragedies.

1 3. It turns friendship into hatred; it makes a man lose himself, and his reason, and his argument, in disputation. It turns the desires of knowledge into an itch of wrangling. It adds insolency to power. It turns justice into cruelty, and judgment into oppression. It changes discipline into tediousness and hatred of liberal institution. It makes a prosperous man to be envied, and the unfortunate to be unpitied. It is a confluence of all the irregular passions: there is in it envy and sorrow, fear and scorn, pride and prejudice, rashness and inconsideration, rejoicing in evil and a desire to inflict it, self-love, impatience, and curiosity. And, lastly, though it be very troublesome to others, yet it is most troublesome to him that hath it.

Be diligent to observe lest, in your desires to suppress anger, you be passionate and angry at yourself for being angry; like physicians who give a bitter potion when they intend to eject the bitterness of choler, for this will provoke the person and increase the passion. But placidly and quietly set upon the mortification of it, and attempt it first for a day, resolving that day not at all to be angry, and to be watchful and observant; for a day is no great trouble: but then, it will be as easy to watch two days, and so you may increase till it becomes easy and habitual.

Anger alone is criminal which is against charity to myself or my neighbour; but anger against sin is a holy zeal, and an effect of love to God and my brother, for whose interest I am passionate, like a concerned person; and if I take care that my anger makes no reflection of scorn or cruelty upon the offender, or of pride and violence, anger becomes charity and duty. And when one commended Charilaus the king of Sparta for a gentle, a good, and a meek prince, his colleagues said well, 'How can he be good who is not an enemy even to vicious persons?'

4 Against covetousness, the third enemy of mercy

Covetousness is also an enemy to alms, though not to all the effects of mercifulness; but this is to be cured by the proper motives to charity before mentioned and the proper rules of justice; which being secured, the arts of getting money are not easily made criminal.

1. Covetousness makes a man miserable, because riches are not

means to make a man happy; and unless felicity were to be bought with money, he is a vain person who admires heaps of gold and rich possessions. They were excellent things, if the richest man were certainly the wisest and the best; but some men choose to be miserable, that they may be rich, rather than be happy with the expense of money and doing noble things.

2. Beyond our needs and conveniences, nature knows no use of riches. No man can, with all the wealth in the world, buy so much skill as to be a good lutenist; he must go the same way that poor people do, he must learn and take pains: much less can he buy constancy or chastity or courage; and by possessing more than we need, we cannot obtain so much power over our own souls as not to require more. And certainly riches must deliver me from no evil, if the possession of them cannot take away the longing for them. If any man be thirsty, drink cools him; if he be hungry, eating meat satisfies him; and when a man is cold, and calls for a warm cloak, he is pleased if you give it him; but you trouble him if you load him with six or eight cloaks. Nature rests, and sits still, when she hath her portion; but that which exceeds it is a trouble and a burden. When God hath satisfied those needs which He made, whatsoever is beyond it is thirst and a disease; and, unless it be sent back again in charity or religion, can serve no end but vice or vanity. No wealth can satisfy the covetous desire of wealth.

3. Riches are troublesome; but the satisfaction of those appetites, which God and nature hath made, are cheap and easy. When we covet after houses, or long for jewels, or for my next neighbour's field, or the richest perfumes of Arabia, then we can never be satisfied till we have the best thing that is fancied, and all that can be had, and desired, and that we can lust no more. But before we come to the one half of our first wild desires, we are the bondmen of userers, and of our worst tyrant appetites, and the tortures of envy and impatience. Those who drink on still when their thirst is quenched, or eat after they have well dined are forced to vomit not only their superfluity, but even that which at first was necessary: so those that covet more than they can temperately use, are oftentimes forced to part even with that patrimony which would have supported their persons in

freedom and honour, and have satisfied all their reasonable desire.

4. Contentedness is therefore health, because covetousness is a direct sickness. Give to a poor man a house, and a few cows, pay his little debt, and set him on work, and he is provided for. No man can desire beyond his bellyful; and, when he wants that, any one friend or charitable man can cure his poverty, but all the world cannot satisfy his covetousness.

5. Covetousness is the most fantastical and contradictory disease in the whole world; it must therefore be incurable, because it strives against its own cure. No man therefore abstains from meat, because he is hungry; nor from wine, because he loves it; and needs it: but the covetous man does so, for he desires it passionately, because he says he needs it, and when he hath it, he will need it still, because he dares not use it. It stirs up the desire, and takes away the pleasure of being satisfied. It increases the appetite, and will not content it: disturbing the order of nature, and the designs of God; making money not to be the instrument of exchange or charity, nor corn to feed himself or the poor, nor wool to clothe himself or his brother, nor wine to refresh the sadness of the afflicted, nor his oil to make his own countenance cheerful; but all these to look upon, and to tell over, and to take accounts by, and make himself considerable, and wondered at by fools; that while he lives he may be called rich. But thus the ass carried wood and sweet herbs to the baths, but was never washed or perfumed himself: he heaped up sweets for others, while himself was filthy with smoke and ashes. Yet if the man can be content to feed hardly, and labour extremely, and watch carefully, and suffer affronts and disgrace, that he may get money more than he uses in his temperate and just needs, with how much ease might this man be happy? And with how great uneasiness and trouble does he make himself miserable? For he takes pains to get content, and when he might have it he lets it go. He might better be content with a virtuous and quiet poverty. The same diet and a less labour would, at first, make him happy, and, for ever after, rewardable.

6. The sum of all is that which the apostle says, 'Covetousness is idolatry'; that is, it is an admiring money for itself, not for its use, it relies upon money, and loves it more than it loves God and religion:

and it is 'the root of all evil'; it teaches men to be cruel and crafty, industrious in evil, full of care and malice; it devours young heirs, and grinds the face of the poor, and undoes those who specially belong to God's protection, helpless, craftless, and innocent people; it inquires into our parent's age, and longs for the death of our friends; it makes friendship an art of rapine, and changes a partner into a vulture, and a companion into a thief; and, after all this, it is for no good to itself; for it dares not spend those heaps of treasure which it snatched: and men hate serpents worse than lions and bears; for these kill because they need the prey, but those sting to death and eat not. And if they pretend all this care and heap for their heirs, why cannot they be without it, as well as their fathers, who did not use it? However, the father transmits it to the son, and it may be the son to one more; till a tyrant, or an oppressor, or a war, or change of government, or the usurer, or folly, or an expensive vice, makes holes in the bottom of the bag, and the wealth runs out like water, and flies away like a bird from the hand of a child.

7. Poverty is a state freer from temptation; a state of which Christ was pleased to make open profession, and many wise men daily make vows. A rich man is but like a pool, to whom the poor run, and first trouble it, and then draw it dry; that he enjoys no more of it than according to the few and limited needs of a man. These considerations may be useful to the curing of covetousness: that the grace of mercifulness enlarging the heart of a man, his hand may not be contracted, but reached out to the poor in alms.

IX OF REPENTANCE

Repentance, of all things in the world, makes the greatest change: it changes things in heaven and earth; for it changes the whole man from sin to grace, from vicious habits to holy customs, from un-chaste bodies to angelical souls, from swine to philosophers, from drunkenness to sober counsels; and God himself throws the records of shame and sorrow from the court of heaven, and lifts up the sinner from the grave to life, from his prison to a throne, from guilt to never-ceasing felicities.

But repentance contains in it all the parts of a holy life, from the time of our return to the day of our death inclusively; and it hath in it some things specially relating to the sins of our former days, now to be abolished by special acts, and special labours. And because it is a duty consisting of so many parts and so much employment, it also requires much time, and is his restitution to the state of righteousness and holy living, for which we covenanted in baptism. There is but one repentance in a man's whole life, if repentance be taken in the proper and strict evangelical covenant sense, and not after the ordinary understanding of the world: we are but once to change our whole state of life, from the power of the devil and the state of sin and death, to the life of grace, to the possession of Jesus, to the kingdom of the gospel; and this is done in the baptism of water, or in the baptism of the Spirit by God's grace coming upon us, and by our obedience to the heavenly calling, we working together with God. After this change, if ever we fall into the contrary state, and be wholly estranged from God and religion, and profess ourselves servants of unrighteousness, God hath made no more covenant to us; there is no place left for any more repentance or new birth; such are voluntary malicious apostates, witches, obstinate impenitent persons, and the like. But if we be overtaken by infirmity, or enter into the marches or borders of this estate, and commit a grievous sin, so we be not in the entire possession of the devil, we are for the present, in a damnable condition if we die; but if we live, we are in a recoverable condition; for so we may repent often. We repent or rise from death but once, but from sickness many times; and by the grace of God we shall be pardoned, if so we repent.

Acts and parts of repentance
1. He that repents truly, is greatly sorrowful for his past sins: not with a superficial sigh or tear, but a pungent, afflictive sorrow; such a sorrow as hates the sin so much, that the man would choose to die rather than act it any more. This sorrow is called in Scripture 'weeping sorely', a 'sorrow of heart', a 'breaking of the spirit', and we may read the degree and manner of it by the lamentations and sad accents of the prophet Jeremy, when he wept for the sins of the nation; by

the heartbreaking of David, when he mourned for his murder and
adultery; and the bitter weeping of St. Peter, after the shameful deny-
ing of his Master. The expression of this sorrow differs according to
the temper of the body, the sex, the age, and circumstance of action,
and the motive of sorrow, and by many accidental tendernesses, or
masculine hardnesses; and the repentance is not to be estimated by
the tears, but by the grief; and the grief is to be valued not by the
sensitive trouble, but by the cordial hatred of the sin, and ready actual
dereliction of it, and a resolution and real resisting its conseque nt
temptations. Some people can shed tears for nothing, some for anything; but the proper and true efforts of a godly sorrow are: fear of
the Divine judgments, apprehension of God's displeasure, watchings
and strivings against sin, patiently enduring the cross of sorrow, in
accusation of ourselves, in perpetually begging pardon, in mean and
base opinions of ourselves, according to our temper and constitution.
For if we be apt to weep in other accidents, it is ill if we weep not
also in the sorrows of repentance; not that weeping is of itself a duty,
but that the sorrow, if it be as great, will be still expressed in as great
a manner.

2. We have no particular measures of sins; we know not which is
greater, of sacrilege or superstition, idolatry or covetousness,
rebellion or witchcraft; but only that a great sin have a great grief, a
smaller crime being to be washed off with a lesser shower.

3. Our sorrow for sins is then best accounted of when it, together
with all the afflictive duties of repentance, shall have equalled or
exceeded the pleasure we had in the sin.

4. True repentance acts its sorrow; and judges and condemns the
sin by judging ourselves, and punishing our bodies and our spirits by
such instruments of piety as are troublesome to the body; such as are
fasting, long prayers, expensive alms, and all outward acts of humiliation. For he that must judge himself, must condemn himself if he be
guilty. This is but the introduction to repentance.

5. Confession of sins hath a special promise: 'If we confess our
sins, He is faithful and just to forgive us our sins'.[36] For confession of
our sins to God is a laying open our wounds for cure. We may very
much be helped if we take in the assistance of a spiritual guide, there-

fore the Church of God in all ages hath commended, and in most ages enjoined, that we confess our sins, and discover the state and condition of our souls to such a person as we or our superiors may judge fit to help us in such needs. For so 'if we confess our sins one to another', as St. James advises, we shall obtain the prayers of the holy man whom God and the Church have appointed; and when he knows our needs, he can best minister comfort or reproof, oil or caustics; and judge better for you than you do for yourself. And this course was taken by the new converts in the days of the apostles: 'For many that believed came and confessed and shewed their deeds'.[37]

6. True repentance must enter into and run through the state of holy living,[38] which is contrary to that state of darkness in which in times past we walked. For to resolve to do it, and yet not to do it, is to break our resolution and our faith, to make our pardon hopeless, and our hope fruitless. He that resolves to live well when a danger is upon him, or a violent fear, or when the appetites of lust are newly satisfied, or newly served, and yet when the temptation comes again, sins again, and then is sorrowful, and resolves once more against it, and yet falls when the temptation returns, is a vain man, but no true penitent. For resolution signifies nothing but in order to the actions: it is as spring is to harvest, as eggs are to birds, nothing without it. No man, therefore, can be in a state of grace and actual favour by resolutions and holy purposes; these are but the gate and portal towards pardon: a holy life is the only perfection of repentance, and the firm ground upon which we can cast the anchor of hope in the mercies of God through Jesus Christ.

7. Man is to begin in hopes according as sin dies in him, and grace lives; as the habits of sin lessen, and righteousness grows. As we return to God, so God returns to us, and our state returns to the probabilities of pardon.

8. Every man is to work out his salvation with fear and trembling.

9. A true penitent must, all the days of his life, pray for pardon, and never think the work completed till he dies; and then those beginnings of pardon, which are working all the way, will at last be perfected in the day of the Lord.

10. Defer not to repent; much less mayest thou put it off to thy

death-bed. It is not an easy thing to root out the habits of sin. We find work enough to mortify one beloved lust, when the work is so great and the strength so little. Repentance being the renewing of a holy life, a living the life of grace, it is a contradiction to say that a man can live a holy life upon his death-bed.

11. After the beginnings of thy recovery, observe where thy failings were, and arm against that temptation. For if all those arguments which God uses to us to preserve our innocence; thy fears, the goodness of God making thee once to escape, the shame of thy fall, and the sense of thy own weaknesses, will not make thee watchful against a fall, especially knowing how much it costs a man to be restored, it will be infinitely more dangerous if ever thou fallest again. Thy own hopes will be made more desperate, thy impatience greater, thy shame turn to impudence, and thy own will be more estranged, violent and refractory, and thy latter end will be worse than thy beginning.

Motives to repentance

I shall use no other arguments to move a sinner to repentance, but to tell him, if he does repent timely and entirely, that is, live a holy life, he shall be forgiven and be saved. Remember,

1. That to admit mankind to repentance and pardon, was a favour greater than ever God gave to the angels and devils; for they were never admitted to the condition of second thoughts: But this Christ did for us: He paid the score of our sins, that we might repent, and that this repentance might be effectual to the great purposes of felicity and salvation.

2. 'For He ever liveth to make intercession for us'.[39] And that we may know what it is in behalf of which He intercedes, St. Paul tells us 'We are ambassadors for Christ, as though He did beseech you by us, we pray you in Christ's stead to be reconciled to God'.[40] And what Christ prays us to do, He prays to God that we may do; that which He desires of us as His servants, He desires of God, who is the fountain of the grace and powers, and without whose assistance we can do nothing.

3. Our blessed Saviour tells us, 'there shall be joy in heaven over

one sinner that repenteth';[41] this is the joy of our Lord, the answering
of His prayers, the satisfaction of His desires, and the reward of His
sufferings, in the repentance and consequent pardon of a sinner. For
therefore He once suffered, and for that reason He rejoices for ever.
When a penitent sinner comes, it is called 'an entering into the joy of
our Lord'; that is, a partaking of that joy which Christ received at our
conversion and enjoyed ever since.

4. The rewards of heaven are so great and glorious, Christ's burden
is so light, his yoke is so easy, that it is a shameless impudence to
expect so great glories at a less service, than a holy life. It cost the
heart-blood of the Son of God to obtain heaven for us upon that
condition; and who shall die again to get heaven for us upon easier
terms? What would you do, if God should command you to kill your
eldest son, or to work in the mines for a thousand years together, or
to fast all thy life-time with bread and water? Were not heaven a very
great bargain even after all this? And when God requires nothing of
us but to live soberly, justly, and godly (which things themselves are
to a man a very great felicity, and necessary to our present well-
being), shall we think this to be an intolerable burden, and that
heaven is too little a purchase at that price; and that God, in mere
justice, will take a death-bed sign or groan, and a few unprofitable
tears and promises, in exchange for all our duty?

If these motives, joined together with our own interest (even as
much as felicity), will not move us to leave the filthiness — and the
trouble — and the uneasiness — and the unreasonableness of sin, and
turn to God, — there is no more to be said; we must perish in our
folly.

X OF PREPARATION TO THE HOLY SACRAMENT OF THE LORD'S SUPPER

The celebration of the holy sacrament is the great mysteriousness of
the Christian religion.

It is the copy of the passion, and the ministration of the great
mystery of our redemption. This celebration is our manner of apply-

ing or using it. The following rules represent preparation:

1. No man must dare to approach to the holy sacrament of the Lord's supper unless in the state of repentance, that is, of sorrow and amendment; lest it be said as it was concerning Judas, the hand of him that betrayeth Me is with Me on the table: and he that receiveth Christ into an impure soul or body, first turns his most excellent nourishment into poison, and then feeds upon it.

2. Every communicant must first have examined the state of his soul, searched out the secret ulcers, weaknesses and indiscretions, and where it is exposed to temptation; that, by finding out its diseases, he may find a cure, secure his present purpose of future amendment, and be armed against dangers and temptations.

3. This examination must be a man's own act and inquisition into his life; it should lead a man on to those whom the great Physician of our souls, Christ Jesus, hath appointed to minister; that in all dangers and great accidents we may be assisted for comfort and remedy, for medicine and caution.

4. Let no man weep for his sins by way of solemnity and ceremony, and still retain the affection: but he that comes to this feast must have on the wedding garment, that is, he must have put on Jesus Christ, and put off the old man with his affections and lusts; and he must be wholly conformed to Christ in the image of his mind. We have put on Christ when every faculty of our soul is proportioned and vested according to the pattern of Christ's life. But to receive it into an unhallowed soul and body will not convey Christ to us, but the devil will enter and dwell there, till with it he returns to his dwelling of torment. This sacrament can no otherwise be celebrated but upon the same terms on which we may hope for pardon and heaven itself.

5. We are to make our souls more adorned; time is specially to be spent in actions of repentance, confession of our sins, renewing our purposes of holy living, praying for those graces which may prevent the like sadnesses for the time to come, meditation upon the passion, and upon the infinite love of God; and in all acts of virtue which may build our souls up into a temple fit for the reception of Christ himself and the inhabitation of the Holy Spirit.

6. The celebration of the Holy Sacrament must suppose us in the love of God and in charity with all the world; and therefore before every communion especially, remember what differences or jealousies are between us and any one else, and recompose all disunions, and cause right understandings between each other; offering to satisfy whom we have injured, and to forgive them who have injured us, without thoughts of resuming the quarrel when the solemnity is over; for that is but to rake the embers in light and fantastic ashes: it must be quenched, and a holy flame enkindled no — fires must be at all, but the fires of love and zeal.

7. When the day of the feast is come, lay aside all cares and impertinences of the world, and remember that this is thy soul's day, a day of traffic and intercourse with Heaven. Arise early in the morning. (1) Give God thanks for the approach of so great a blessing. (2) Confess thine own unworthiness to admit so divine a guest. (3) Then remember and deplore thy sins, which have made thee so unworthy. (4) Then confess God's goodness, and take sanctuary there, and upon Him place thy hopes; (5) And invite Him to thee with renewed acts of love, of holy desire, of hatred of His enemy, sin. (6) Make oblation of thyself wholly to His providence and possession, and pray Him to enter and dwell there for ever. And after this, with joy and holy fear, address thyself to the receiving of Him, to whom, and by whom, all faith and all hope, and all love, in the holy Catholic Church, both in heaven and earth, is designed; Him, whom kings and queens, and whole kingdoms are in love with, and count it the greatest honour in the world that their crowns and sceptres are laid at his feet.

8. When the holy man ministers the rite of consecration, then do as the angels do, who behold, and love, and wonder that the Son of God should become food to the souls of His servants; that by his death He should bring thee to life, and by becoming a man He should make thee partaker of the Divine nature. These are such glories that, although they are made so obvious that each eye may behold them, yet they are also so deep that no thought can fathom them: but so it hath pleased Him to make these mysteries to be sensible, because the excellency and depth of the mercy is not intelligible; that

while we are ravished and comprehended within the infiniteness of so vast and mysterious a mercy, yet we may be as sure of it as of that thing we see and feel, and smell and taste; but yet it is so great that we cannot understand it.

9. These holy mysteries are offered to our senses; they are sensible, but not common: and as the weakness of the elements adds wonder to the excellency of the sacrament, so let our reverence and reverent usages of them add honour to the elements, and acknowledge the glory of the mystery, and the Divinity of the mercy. Let us receive the consecrated elements with all devotion and humility of body and spirit; and do this honour to it, that it be the first food we eat, and the first beverage we drink that day, unless it be in sickness, or other great necessity; and that your body and soul both be prepared to its reception with abstinence from secular pleasures, that you may better have attended fastings and preparatory prayers. For if ever it be seasonable to observe the counsel of St. Paul, that married persons by consent should abstain for a time, that they may attend to solemn religion, it is now. It was not by St. Paul, nor the after-ages of the Church, called a duty so to do, but it is most reasonable that the more solemn actions of religion should be attended to, without the mixture of anything that may discompose the mind.

10. In the act of receiving, exercise acts of faith: believe thou dost verily receive Christ's body and blood to all effects and purposes of the Spirit. Dispute not concerning the secret of the mystery; it is sufficient to thee that Christ shall be present to thy soul as an instrument of grace, as a pledge of the resurrection, as the earnest of glory and immortality, and a means of many blessings, all such as are necessary for Thee and in order to thy salvation. And to make all this good to thee, there is nothing necessary on thy part but a holy life, and a true belief of all the sayings of Christ. Believe that Christ, in the holy sacrament, gives thee His body and His blood. He that believes not this is not a Christian. He that believes so much needs not to enquire further, not to entangle his faith by disbelieving his sense.

11. Fail not at this solemnity, to make an offering to God for the uses of religion and the poor, according to thy ability. If thou

chancest to communicate where this holy custom is not observed
publicly, supply that want by thy private charity.

12. When you have received, pray and give thanks. Pray for all
estates of men; and you, with Christ (whom then you have received),
are more fit to pray for them in the celebration of that holy sacrifice,
which then is sacramentally re-presented to God.

13. After the solemnity is done, let Christ dwell in your hearts by
faith, and love, and obedience, and conformity to His life and death.
Remember, that now Christ is all one with you; and, therefore, when
you are to do an action consider how Christ did, or would do the
like; and do you imitate His example, and marry His loves and
hatreds, and contract His friendships; for then do you every day communicate; Christ thus dwells in you, and you in Christ.

14. Do not instantly, upon your return from church, return also to
secular thoughts and employment; but let the remaining parts of that
day be like a post-communion, entertaining your blessed Lord with
all the caresses and sweetness of love, of duty and affection, acquaint-
ing Him with all your needs, all your secrets, and all your infirmities;
and as the affairs of your person or employment call you off, so retire
again to your beloved guest.

The effects and benefits of worthy communicating

The church is nourished in her faith, strengthened in her hope, en-
larged with increasing charity; there all the members of Christ are
joined with each other, and all to Christ their head; and we again
renew the covenant with God in Jesus Christ, and God seals His part,
and we promise for ours, and Christ unites both, and the Holy Ghost
signs both in the collation of those graces which we then pray for,
and exercise, and receive all at once. There our bodies are nourished
with the signs, and our souls with the mystery: our bodies receive
into them the seed of an immortal nature, and our souls are joined
with Him who is the first-fruits of the resurrection and never can die.
And if we desire anything else and need it, here it is to be prayed for,
here to be hoped for, here to be received. Long life and health, and
recovery from sickness, and competent support and maintenance,
and peace and deliverance from our enemies, and content, and

patience, and joy, and sanctified riches, or a cheerful poverty, and
liberty, and whatsoever else is a blessing. If we receive worthily, we
shall receive any of these blessings, according as God shall choose for
us; and He will not only choose with more wisdom, but also with
more affection, than we can for ourselves.

After all this, it is advised by the guides of souls, wise men and
pious, that all persons should communicate very often, even as often
as they can without excuses or delays. All Christian people must
come. They, indeed that are in the state of sin must first quit their
state of death, and then partake of the bread of life. They that are at
enmity with their neighbours must come, only they must leave their
enmity and then come. They that have variety of secular employment
must leave their secular thoughts and affections behind them, and
then come and converse with God. If any man be well grown in
grace, he must needs come, because he is excellently disposed to so
holy a feast; but he that is but in the infancy of piety had need to
come, that so he may grow in grace. The strong must come lest they
become weak; and the weak that they may become strong. The sick
must come to be cured; the healthful to be preserved. They that have
leisure must come, because they have no excuse; they that have no
leisure must come hither, that by so excellent religion they may
sanctify their business. The penitent sinners must come, that they may
be justified. So our souls may be transformed into the similitude and
union with Christ by our perpetual feeding on Him, and conversation
not only in His courts, but in His very heart, and most secret affections, and incomparable purities.

Preparation to receiving the blessed sacrament of the Lord's Supper
The just preparation to this holy feast consisting principally in a holy
life, the acts of all virtues, and especially of faith, repentance, charity,
and thanksgiving; to the exercise of these four graces, let the person
that intends to communicate, set times apart for his preparation and
devotions.

An act of love
O eternal God, helper of the helpless, comforter of the comfortless, hope of the afflicted,

bread of the hungry, drink of the thirsty, and Saviour of all them that wait upon Thee; I bless and glorify Thy name, and adore Thy goodness, and delight in Thy love. Take from me all affection to sin or vanity; let my affections soar upwards to the element of love, that I may hunger and thirst for the bread of life, and the wine of elect souls, and know no love but the love of God. Amen.

An act of desire
Lord Jesus, come quickly; my heart is desirous of Thy presence, and would entertain Thee, not as a guest, but as an inhabitant, as the Lord of all my faculties. Enter in and take possession, and dwell with me for ever, that I also may dwell in the heart of my dearest Lord, which was opened for me with a spear and love.

An act of contrition
Lord, Thou shalt find my heart full of cares and worldly desires, neglect of holy things, proud and crafty to deceive itself, entangled with difficult cases of conscience, with knots which my own wildness, inconsideration and impatience have tied. O Lord, the place to which Thou art invited is full of passion and prejudice, evil principles and evil habits, peevish and disobedient, lustful and intemperate. I am heartily ashamed, and truly sorrowful for it, and do deeply hate all my sins, and humbly beg of Thee to increase my sorrow, care, and hatred against sin; and make my love to Thee swell up to a great grace, to glory and immensity.

An act of faith
Thou didst take upon Thee my nature, and Thou didst suffer to deliver me from my sins that I might serve Thee in holiness and righteousness all my days. Lord, I am as sure Thou didst the great work of redemption for me and all mankind, as that I am alive. This is my hope, the strength of my spirit, my joy and my confidence; and do Thou never let the spirit of unbelief enter into me and take me from this rock. Here I dwell, for I have a delight therein; here I will live, and here I desire to die.

The petition
O blessed Jesu, enter into my heart, and cast out all impurities; grant I may partake of this holy sacrament with much reverence, and great effect, for the establishment of an unreproveable faith, of an unfeigned love, for the fulness of wisdom, for the healing of my soul, for the blessing and preservation of my body, for the ejection of all evil from within me, and the fulfilling of all Thy righteous commandments.

To be said before or at the receiving the Holy Sacrament
Like as the heart desireth the water-brooks, so longeth my soul after Thee, O God. My
soul is athirst for God, yea, even for the living God: when shall I come before the
presence of God? Psal. xlii. 1, 2

O send out Thy light and Thy truth, that they may lead me, and bring me unto Thy
holy hill and to Thy dwelling; and that I may go unto the altar of God, even unto the
God of my joy and gladness; and with my heart will I give thanks to Thee, O God my
God. Psal. xliii. 3, 4

I will wash my hands in innocency, O Lord, and so will I go to Thine altar: that I
may shew the voice of thanksgiving, and tell of all Thy wondrous works. Psal. xxvi.
6, 7

Examine me, O Lord, and prove me, try Thou my reins and my heart. For Thy
loving-kindness is now and ever before my eyes: and I will walk in Thy truth. Psal.
xxvi. 2, 3

Thou shalt prepare a table before me against them that trouble me: Thou hast
annointed my head with oil, and my cup shall be full. But Thy loving-kindness and
mercy shall follow me all the days of my life, and I will dwell in the house of the
Lord for ever. Psal. xxiii. 5, 6

This is the bread that cometh down from heaven, that a man may eat thereof and not
die. John vi. 50

Whoso eateth My flesh, and drinketh My blood, dwelleth in Me and I in him, and
hath eternal life abiding in him; and I will raise him up at the last day. Ver. 54, 56

Lord, whither shall we go but to Thee? Thou hast the words of eternal life.
Ver. 68

If any man thirst, let him come unto me and drink. John vii. 37

The bread which we break, is it not the communication of the body of Christ? and the
cup which we drink, is it not the communication of the blood of Christ? 1 Cor. x. 16

What are those wounds in thy hands? They are those with which I was wounded in
the house of my friends. Zech. xii. 6

Immediately before the receiving say,
Lord, I am not worthy that Thou shouldest enter under my roof, But do Thou speak
the word only, and Thy servant shall be healed. Matt. viii. 8

Lord, open Thou my lips, and my mouth shall shew Thy praise. O God, make speed
to save me: O Lord, make haste to help me.

Come, Lord Jesus, come quickly.

After receiving, say,

Be Thou Lord of all my faculties. O let me feed on Thee by faith, and grow up by the increase of God to a perfect man in Christ Jesus. Amen. Lord, I believe: help mine unbelief.

Glory be to God the Father, Son, &c.

It is finished. Blessed be the mercies of God revealed to us in Jesus Christ. Let the sacrifice of the cross, which Thou didst once offer for the sins of the whole world obtain mercy and peace, faith and charity, safety and establishment to Thy holy Church; and let not the gates of hell prevail against her, nor the enemy of mankind take any soul out of Thy hand. Preserve all Thy people from heresy and division of spirit, from scandal and the spirit of delusion, from sacrilege and hurtful persecutions. Keep me for ever in holy living, from sin and sinful shame, in the communion of Thy Church, and Thy Church in safety and grace, in truth and peace. Amen.

Dearest Jesu, be jealous of Thy house and the place where Thine honour dwelleth. Teach me so to walk, that I may never disrepute the honour of my religion, nor stain the holy robe which Thou hast now put upon my soul, nor break my holy vows. Make me to serve Thee in the communion of saints, in receiving the sacrament, in the practice of all holy virtues, in the imitation of Thy life, and conformity to Thy sufferings: that I, having now put on the Lord Jesus, may marry His loves and His enmities, may desire His glory, and may obey His laws, and be united to His spirit, and in the day of the Lord I may be found having on the wedding garment, and bearing in my body and soul the marks of the Lord Jesus, that I may enter into the joy of my Lord, and partake of His glories for ever and ever. Amen.

Prayers for all sorts of men and all necessities

A Prayer to be said in any affliction, in a sad and disconsolate spirit, and in temptations to despair

O eternal God, Father of mercies, and God of all comfort, with much mercy look upon the sadness and sorrows of Thy servant. The waters are gone over me, and my miseries are without comfort. Lord, pity me! Let Thy grace refresh my spirit! Let Thy comforts support me, Thy mercy pardon me, and never let my portion be amongst hopeless spirits. I can need no relief so great as Thy mercy is; for Thou art infinitely more merciful that I can be miserable; and Thy mercy far above my misery. Dearest Jesus, let me trust in Thee for ever, and let me never be counfounded. Amen

Short Prayers to be said by sick persons

O holy Jesus, Thou art touched with the sense of our infirmities; Thou knowest the sharpness of my sickness, and the weakness of my person. Let Thy mercy support me, Thy spirit guide me, and lead me through the valley of this death safely; that I may pass it patiently, holily, with perfect resignation; and let me rejoice in the Lord, in the hopes of pardon, in the expectation of glory, in the sense of Thy mercies, in the refreshments of Thy Spirit, in a victory over all temptations.

Thou hast promised to be with us in tribulation: Lord, my soul is troubled, and my body is weak, and my hope is in Thee; let Thy hand of grace be upon me: restrain my ghostly enemies, and give me all sorts of spiritual assistances.

Take me from all tediousness of spirit, all impatiency and unquietness: let me possess my soul in patience, and resign my soul and body into the hands of a faithful Creator and a blessed Redeemer.

O holy Jesu, Thou didst die for us; by Thy sad, pungent, and intolerable pains, which Thou enduredst for me, have pity on me, and ease my pain, or increase my patience. Lay on me no more than Thou shalt enable me to bear. Lord, I am weak, and I fear lest something should happen that may discompose the state of my soul, that may displease Thee: preserve me in Thy fear and favour, that nothing may be able to separate me from the love of God in Jesus Christ. O Lord, smite me friendly, for Thou knowest my infirmities. Into Thy hands I commend my spirit; for Thou hast redeemed me, O Lord, thou God of truth. Come, Holy Spirit, help me in this conflict. Come, Lord Jesus, come quickly.

Acts of hope, to be used by sick persons after a pious life

I am persuaded, that neither death, nor life, nor angels, nor principalities, nor powers, nor things present, nor things to come, nor height, nor depth, nor any other creature, shall be able to separate me from the love of God, which is in Christ Jesus our Lord. Rom. viii. 38, 39

I have fought a good fight: I have finished my course: I have kept the faith. Henceforth there is laid up for me a crown of righteousness, which the Lord, the righteous judge, shall give me at that day; and not to me only, but unto all them also that love His appearing. 2 Tim. iv. 7, 8

Blessed be God, even the Father of our Lord Jesus Christ, the Father of mercies and the God of all comfort, who comforts us in all our tribulation. 2 Cor. i. 3, 4

A Prayer to be said in behalf of a sick or dying person

Lord, look upon him with much mercy and pity, forgive him all his sins, comfort his sorrows, ease his pain, satisfy his doubts, relieve his fears, instruct his ignorances, strengthen his understanding, take from him all disorders of spirit, weakness and abuse of fancy. Restrain the malice and power of the spirits of darkness; and suffer him to be injured neither by his ghostly enemies nor his own infirmities; and let a holy and just peace, the peace of God, be within his conscience.

Lord, preserve his senses till the last of his time, strengthen his faith, confirm his hope, and give him a never-ceasing charity to Thee, and to all the world: stir up in him contrition for all the evils he hath done, and give him patience for all he suffers: give him prudence, memory, and consideration, rightly to state the accounts of his soul; and do Thou remind him of all his duty, that when it shall please Thee that his soul goes out from the prison of his body, it may be preserved from the surprise of evil spirits, for ever to live, and to behold the face of God in the glories of the Lord Jesus, our blessed and ever-glorious Redeemer. Amen.

A Prayer before a journey

O Almighty God, who fillest all things with Thy presence, and art a God afar off as well as near at hand; guide me in my journey, preserving me from dangers of robbers, violence of enemies, sudden and sad accidents, falls and errors. Prosper my journey to Thy glory, and to all my innocent purposes. Preserve me from all sin, that I may return in peace and holiness, and may serve Thee in thankfulness and obedience all the days of my pilgrimage; and at last bring me to Thy country, to dwell in Thy house, and to sing praises to Thee for ever. Amen.

NOTES: CHAPTER 4

1 James I^{27}
2 Titus II^{12}
3 2 Cor. XIII^5 Rom. VIII^{10}
4 Heb. II^{18}
5 1 Cor. XIII
6 Gal. IV^{18}
7 Rom. X^2
8 Titus II^{14} Rev. III^{16}
9 2 Cor. VII^{11}
10 Rom. XII^1
11 Luke XVI$^{29, \ 31}$
12 Luke XXIV^{45} Matt. XXII^{29} Acts
     XV^{21} 2 Tim. III^{16} Rev. I^3
13 1 John III^{22} John IX^{31} Isa. I^{15}
     LVIII^5 Mal. III^{10} 1 Tim. II^8
     Psalm XXXIV^{16} LXVI^{18}
14 Mark XI^{24} James I$^{6, \ 7}$
15 Rom. XII^{12} XV^{20} Col. IV^{12}
     1 Thess. III^{10} Ephes. VI^{18}
16 1 Peter IV^7
17 James V$^{16, \ 17}$
18 Luke XVIII^1 XXI^{36}
19 1 Thess. V^{17}
20 Phil. IV^6
21 1 Tim. II^8
22 1 Tim. II$^{1-3}$

23 Matt. XXV^{35}
24 Matt. XXVI^{12} 2 Sam. II^5
25 Heb. X^{24}
26 1 Thess. V^{14}
27 2 Cor. IX^7
28 Luke VI^{30} Gal. VI ^{10}
29 Luke XII^2 Acts III^6
30 1 Peter I^{22}
31 2 Cor. VIII^{12}
32 Matt. VI^4 XII^{33} XXV^{45}
     Luke XI^{41}
33 Phil. IV^{17}
34 Acts X^4 Heb. XIII^{16} Dan. IV^{27}
35 Col. III^{12}
36 1 John I^9
37 Acts XIX^{18}
38 Rom. VI$^{3, \ 4, \ 7}$ VIII^{10} XI$^{22, \ 27}$
     XIII$^{13, \ 14}$ Gal. V$^{6, \ 24}$ VI^{15}
     1 Cor. VII^{19} 2 Cor. XIII^5
     Col. I$^{21-23}$ Heb. XII$^{1, \ 14, \ 16}$
     X$^{16-22}$ 1 Peter I^{15} 2 Peter I$^{4, \ 9, \ 10}$
     III^{11} 1 John I^6 III$^{8, \ 9}$ V^{16}
39 Heb. VII^{25}
40 2 Cor. V^{20}
41 Luke XV^7

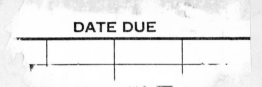

DATE DUE